Adventures in the Wild

Adventures in the Wild

TALES FROM BIOLOGISTS
OF THE NATURAL STATE

Edited by
Joy Trauth and Aldemaro Romero

THE UNIVERSITY OF ARKANSAS PRESS
FAYETTEVILLE   2008

ISBN-10: 1-55728-872-0
ISBN-13: 978-1-55728-872-1

12   11   10   09   08   5   4   3   2   1

Text design by Ellen Beeler

♾ The paper used in this publication meets the minimum
requirements of the American National Standard for Permanence
of Paper for Printed Library Materials Z39.48-1984.

Library of Congress Cataloging-in-Publication Data

Adventures in the wild : tales from biologists of the natural state /
edited by Joy Trauth and Aldemaro Romero.
p. cm.
Includes bibliographical references and index.
ISBN 978-1-55728-872-1 (pbk. : alk. paper)
1. Biology—Fieldwork—Anecdotes. 2. Arkansas State University.
Dept. of Biological Sciences—Officials and employees—Anecdotes.
3. Biologists—Arkansas—Anecdotes. I. Trauth, Joy, 1952–
II. Romero Díaz, Aldemaro.
QH318.5.A38 2008
570.72'3—dc22
2007050669
Printed in Canada

Contents

Foreword

In October 2004 I had the opportunity to visit Arkansas State University. In my position as then director of the National Museum of Natural History, I was invited to speak about the importance of natural history collections. I was impressed by the enthusiasm and professionalism of the faculty of the Department of Biological Sciences, their efforts to document the biodiversity of Arkansas, and their dedication to the growth and maintenance of their collections. I was also pleased to learn about the plans that institution had to build a Biodiversity Center: a modern research and teaching facility where the institution's half a million specimens of plants and animals could be housed together and more effectively utilized.

A year and a half later I received a call from Dr. Aldemaro Romero, chair of the department; he told me that he and a colleague were planning to collect and edit stories written by members of the Department of Biological Sciences about their experiences in the field and laboratory. The goal of the book was twofold: one was to show the public how diverse and interesting field biologists' work is; the second objective was to use the book to raise funds for the building of the Biodiversity Center. Dr. Romero asked me if I would be interested in writing the prologue for the book, and I immediately accepted the invitation.

The stories in the book that Ms. Joy Trauth, an instructor of biology at Arkansas State University, and Dr. Romero compiled illustrate the excitement associated with the field work carried out by biologists around the world every day. The stories reveal the exhilaration felt by biologists when discovering new information and collecting new specimens of plants and animals. The stories also allow the reader to accompany the biologists as they relive challenges and, in some cases, face life-threatening situations.

These experiences will interest and even captivate many of the readers of this and other natural history books, whether they are professional scientists or lay individuals. Although all the authors are professional scientists, they were able to put in clear and understandable language their own scientific experiences.

The chapters of this book also show us how important biological collections are for the understanding and conservation of our natural heritage worldwide. Readers will recognize that behind each specimen of a plant or animal in a museum, there is a personal story of how that specimen was identified, collected, and placed on exhibit.

The reader will find in this book not only a source of amusement, excitement, and intrigue, but also a means of supporting the work that biologists, like the ones working at Arkansas State University, are doing every day to help us understand the natural world and to preserve it for future generations.

Dr. Cristián Samper
Acting Secretary of the Smithsonian Institution
August 2007

Poisonous Plants, Purple Paint, and Pot

STARIA VANDERPOOL

𝒱 MY INTEREST IN plant taxonomy was strongly developed from the fifth grade on, so I had done a lot of field work with plants while I was in high school, and I started college as a major in botany. I had spent years trying to convince my mother that I was not going to poison the family by keeping the refrigerator full of native plants—an assertion reinforced by the fact that no family member had ever shown any signs of toxicity. When I realized that I was going to be isolated on a college campus, restricted to a shared dorm room, and cut off from contact with native plants, I decided to transplant some of my favorite plants to my dorm room. We had great light, and I was rooming with another biology major, so it was feasible.

I established native mint and other wetland plants that thrived in the dorm room. In addition I also transplanted dwarf crested iris, wild violet, and other early spring woodland flowers to the dorm room. My biological reasoning was sound—these were all herbaceous perennials that could survive in reduced light. My roommate and I enjoyed the patch of native wildflowers that I had established in our room during our freshman year.

However, my roommate had developed a persistent skin rash that the campus health center nurse treated with topical creams and other remedies. My roommate was tested for ectoparasites as well as stress-related causes. Her rash would clear up, but would always reappear. It wasn't severe enough to justify seeing a specialist, so she spent the year applying Calamine lotion and other ointments. Everyone was baffled by her skin rash and its failure to respond to treatment.

During our sophomore year I moved to another dorm, taking my transplanted garden with me. My former roommate's skin rash cleared up during her sophomore year, and they concluded it must have been stress-induced. It was only years later, when I took a graduate course in plant metabolites, that I learned that many people have an allergic reaction to *Iris* that presents as a rash. I've never had the courage to track down my friend and confess that I suspect that my native plant garden probably had been the cause of her rash all those years ago.

A sufficiently large percentage of the population is allergic to poison ivy for the effect of contact with the oils from that plant to be well established. Other plants, such as monkshood or castor bean, are well-known poisonous plants. What is less well known is that people can have an idiosyncratic allergic reaction to any of the many different types of secondary compounds that plants produce. In fact, many botanists and physicians don't realize this.

Call it cosmic vengeance or roommate's revenge if you want, but I had my own, much itchier, encounter with innocuous-seeming plants years later. This time I knew enough to realize my mistake minutes after I made it and anticipate potential outcomes for a full forty-eight hours before suffering the consequences.

When you've worked in "the field" in Arkansas for years, you learn to recognize and avoid poison ivy, copperheads, cottonmouths, and rattlesnakes automatically. Over the years, as a professional biologist, I've learned to acknowledge that snakes play a valuable role in the community—but they still get my attention when I stumble, run, or step across one of them. On the other hand, poison ivy is one of the predominate plants in many of the areas where I work, especially in the bottomland hardwood areas I've been working in recently. Since I'm relatively insensitive to poison ivy, I am casual about walking through it or being around it. In fact, there are several poison ivy plants that I have successfully ignored for years in the hedges around my native plant gardens at home.

However, take a field botanist out of his or her local field, combine that with an insatiable curiosity about plants and a certain level of confidence, and the stage is set for a learning experience. My graduate student Linh Hoang and I were working on an investigation of the population genetics of Riddell's goldenrod. For the genetics research we needed representative specimens from throughout the range of the species. Since the range of Riddell's goldenrod extends northward from northern Arkansas to southern Ontario and Manitoba, our field trip took us into unfamiliar biotic regions. As Riddell's goldenrod is usually found in high-quality wetlands, many of the populations we received permission to sample were in state natural areas, parks, or preserves. We had a lot of area to cover, permission to enter and collect plant materials from pristine plant communities, a driver/camp manager in the form of my long-time field partner—my husband—and a CD player/tape deck stocked with tapes prepared by Linh's partner. It was sheer heaven for a trio of rabid field biologists and closet natural history buffs.

Some of the most exciting sites we investigated were the bogs and fens in Wisconsin and Minnesota. When you're surrounded by large populations of pitcher plants, sundews, and pickerel weed (and Riddell's goldenrod—our target species and reason for being there) for the first time, everything else recedes into the background. As we squelched, slithered, and slid across the plants on the periphery of the open bog ponds, I was examining every new plant species we encountered. Bog communities had always fascinated me, but I was familiar with them only through the literature. On one side of the bog there was a faint game trail leading through a stand of small shrubs. I took the game trail—reasoning that would be more stable footing. Then I stopped under the shrubs—because these were new to me too. Woody shrubs, sparsely branched, large compound leaves, bark that had large lenticels—could it be an unfamiliar species of elderberry, or *Rhus*—something besides smooth sumac or shining or winged sumac. Only a careful, hands-on examination would help me identify the plant. Alternate leaves—not an elderberry then. Maybe it was an unfamiliar sumac species. Most plants in the cashew family have a characteristic odor—a little acrid—so I broke a leaf off the plant and started to sniff it. Just then I saw the familiar clusters of small green flowers and white berries and realized that I had just started a close, hands-on investigation of a new sumac species—poison sumac!

I carefully withdrew from the clump of shrubs, washed my face, hands, and arms in bog water—hoping that my relative immunity to poison ivy would hold true for poison sumac—and waited. Well, by the next day there was strong evidence to support the hypothesis that I was not insensitive to poison sumac. I had a full-blown case of poison sumac on my hands, arms, and even on my neck. Everywhere I touched the poison sumac (and remember—I started my identification of this unknown plant by walking into a clump of shrubs), I had blisters. When we got back to the park headquarters, I took the time to study their public information signs about poisonous snakes (none), black widow spiders, black bear, unstable footing, and poison sumac. That's one plant that I will remember —a week of antihistamine creams, cortisone creams, and tea packs ensured that I will never forget what poison sumac looks like.

Those poison ivy plants in my hedges at home are still there. I still ignore them, and, so far, they still ignore me. But I have a new rationale for leaving them there. Now they are a tax write-off, as part of the teaching resources that my home gardens provide for courses that I teach in plant taxonomy, field botany, and economic botany.

Even after becoming a college professor, I had not realized that leading field trips was such a multi-faceted professional challenge until my first few trips with students in plant taxonomy. Certain assumptions about prior knowledge and experience just have to be discarded—along with a certain wishful thinking about common sense and field work. Over the years I have changed and refined my approach to teaching any field botany course.

Now the first field trip of the spring semester is just across town—to the teaching gardens at my house. They include a woodland garden with native spring wildflowers such as dwarf crested iris, bloodroot, wood phlox, purple, white, and yellow violets, and other species. In addition to the herbaceous plants, I also have native shrubs, including vernal witch hazel, spice bush, and pawpaw. In sunny areas I have beds of spring flowering bulbs, medicinal plants, and native prairie species, and the grassy areas are full of winter weeds and other annuals. Altogether, these plantings can be used as field laboratories to introduce plant communities, plant conservation biology principles, collection techniques, common elements of the native flora, and (I'm such an optimist) common sense in the field.

Based on my personal experience with poison sumac, I'm not sure I can justify my assumption that everyone can recognize poison ivy, but the first stop on every field trip is the poison ivy population in the hedges—where we can see the ground herbaceous form, the shrubby form, and the vine form, clinging to the hackberry tree with its characteristic hairy adventitious roots. Mixed in with the poison ivy is Virginia creeper, with five leaflets, which is frequently mistaken for poison ivy.

After the introduction to poison ivy, there is a quick review of the logistics of urban and roadside field collection techniques. If plants are growing inside a square, rectangular, or circular bed—particularly if they have large showy flowers—the chances are very strong that these are not plants native to Arkansas, and therefore not appropriate for a plant collection. Tulips, bearded iris, pansies, grape hyacinths, and other spring-flowering bulbs should not be collected for your plant collection. At best you lose points on your plant collection, at worst you also lose standing with the gardener whose garden you are raiding.

Next we proceed to the spring woodland garden and ramp up the cognitive challenge for the novice field botanists. The boundaries are there, but they are winding rather than being geometric. There is a lot of diversity represented, with over thirty species flowering. Many of these are showy, but some of them have inconspicuous flowers. Many represent species that the students may be familiar with in the wild—such as phlox, trillium, and yellow wood poppy. At this point I can discuss plant taxonomy with an introduction to species of native wildflowers in situ, and I also discuss ethics and plant conservation biology. Some of the plants in my wildflower garden are purchased from reputable native plant nurseries such as Ridgecrest Nursery in Wynne, Arkansas, or Pine Ridge Nursery near Russellville, Arkansas, where plants are guaranteed to be propagated from nursery stock or seed sources and not collected from the wild. Others were collected from our farm in the Ozarks and taken from large, well-established populations that would not be decimated by the removal of rootstock. The third point that I impress on the students is that I can recognize individuals from my garden, and I would associate any holes in my garden with poached plants that show up in their plant collections.

Comparison and contrast is a powerful teaching tool in the field. Once I've established the basis for discriminating between cultivated plants, native plants, and plants in gardens, then I can introduce the class to plants growing in urban settings that are fair game for the novice plant collector. Just outside the beds of cultivated and native plantings is the grassy lawn, decorated (my perspective) or desecrated (the urban lawn fan perspective) by numerous spring flowering annuals and perennials. Many of these are weedy winter annuals such as henbit, deadnettle, chickweed, and plants in the mustard family. Others are native species, such as spring beauty and bluets or perennials such as dandelion, fleabane, buttercups, and violets. The take-home message here is that these plants are appropriate for plant taxonomy collections as long as they get permission from the home owner. Naturally, I am happy to give them permission to collect all the "weeds" from my lawn that they want, as long as they respect the boundaries of the established gardens and avoid collecting from my cherished native plant gardens.

One of the many things I enjoy about being a teaching botany professor is the constant challenge of learning from experience and incorporating new information into my classroom whether I'm in an outdoor setting or in the lab. Before I teach plant taxonomy again, I'm going to make two specific additions to my teaching garden. I'm going to plant an entire plot of buckeye seeds (*Aesculus* species), and I'm going to find a nice Ozark limestone boulder, place it in the shrub border, and paint a splotch of purple paint on the boulder.

Plant taxonomy at Arkansas State University is a spring course, so much of our experience with native plant species comes from weedy species in lawns and waste areas and from woodland communities where there is a mixture of spring ephemeral wildflowers and flowering trees and shrubs. Field trip number two is usually to a wooded area on Crowley's Ridge that is diverse and accessible. Once we reach the area, we have a brief orientation and then the class splits up to explore the area. Since my progress through any plant community has been described as resembling that of a beagle looking for rabbit scent trails (slow, rambling, and with my head down), the students usually range ahead of me.

On one of these trips I was horrified to hear two of my students racing back to me, yelling, "Dr. V., Dr. V., we found marijuana!" My first reaction was that they had found a pot patch—it's not an uncommon find for botanists in a forested area. My second thought was that we could be in serious danger if we had stumbled on a defended pot patch. And my third thought was that I had overlooked yet another element of field work etiquette—the essential need to pretend that you're clueless about the identity of marijuana, even if you do find a population. Fortunately for everyone, the pair had found a population of young red buckeye, which does have palmately compound leaves, so in fact it was a false alarm. It had never occurred to me that any of my students would not recognize marijuana leaves or confuse them with other plants.

So, I've added red buckeye to my gardens, and I make a point of introducing plants with palmately compound leaves—such as buckeye, *Potentilla* species, and *Cleome* species—in lecture or lab. I've added another point to my field etiquette lecture: appropriate behavior when you think you've found a pot patch: pretend that you're clueless, don't recognize the plant, and very, very carefully leave the area without collecting any specimens. Once you're well away from the area and back to your vehicle, then you pack up and get out. Above everything, don't run, shouting "we found marijuana" at the top of your lungs.

Field biology, whether botany, ecology, or zoology, has changed significantly since I was an undergraduate student. Access to private or public property is less readily available. When I started, it was sufficient to respect "No Trespassing" signs and fences on private property. Many public areas such as national forests or wildlife management areas were accessible with verbal permission from the local biologist or ranger. Today private landowners control access to their property. The introduction of laws that allow landowners to mark boundaries with purple boundary paint allowed them to easily expand no trespassing boundaries by substituting a quick burst of spray paint for the laborious task of purchasing and hanging no trespassing signs. Concerns about landowner liability and loss of game, timber, or domestic animals expanded private landowners' caution about permitting biologists on their property. To the modern field biologist, student or professional, that patch of purple paint is as substantial as a five-wire fence and large yellow no trespassing signs. It is essential to receive permission from landowners before entering their property to collect plants. In addition, most animal species are protected and you require collecting permits for non-game animals. One component of every field course has to include the current and relevant guidelines for collecting specimens.

At the same time, public land management agencies became more aware of the need to protect public resources on managed lands. Permitting laws were instituted that control collection of plants or animals from state or federal lands. Acquiring permission for access to a specific site includes knowledge of the state or federal agency, knowledge about rare, threatened, or endangered species whose collection is regulated by federal guidelines, and the multiple permits that may be required for a combination area.

Together, the regulations narrow the natural areas available for students and biologists alike in field courses. They also alter the contextual content of field courses. We are more aware of the need for conservation of natural resources, which includes removal of individuals for classroom use and research purposes. It is no longer adequate to justify general collections solely for field courses to build recognition and identification skills in the student population. Conservation and ethical issues are critical to consider in designing the modern field course. Prior to field work, we have to familiarize ourselves with the identity of sensitive species. The size of populations should be considered, and removal of individuals should only occur if the population is large enough to sustain loss of one or more individuals. As many plants are herbaceous perennials, it is possible to collect stems while leaving the underground perennating structures intact and capable of producing additional stems.

Field biology classes should be designed to incorporate a research context. In plant taxonomy I incorporate plant conservation biology in lecture and in lab. The two sides to plant conservation biology are rare, threatened, or endangered species and invasive species. Much of our lab work utilizes invasive species that are common lawn, roadside, or field species. We can utilize these as "training specimens" for developing technical identification skills, recognition of common elements of the flora, and an assessment of the invasive or nonnative plant species characteristic of a region. Since the hallmark of an invasive species is its mobility, this approach is one strategy for identifying and tracking the progress of invasive or nonnative species.

Another strategy that allows field biologists to continue to incorporate a field element in our classrooms is incorporating a research component in a field course. I have found that combining field experiences for my plant taxonomy students with floristic surveys of area parks or wildlife management areas is a good strategy. When I get permission for us to work in a specific area, students can develop skills for plant surveys and plant collection and identification as well as contribute to a final product that has value for the host agency. The concentrated efforts of twenty or more students in a defined area can result in a comprehensive inventory of plants that can be used by the management agency. Since all students are working in a specific area where I can be involved in their work, then I have confidence in their findings. In addition to the utility of their results to the host agency, their work also becomes data that I can confidently incorporate in the herbarium at Arkansas State University, which I curate. The E. L. Richards Collection was founded by Professor E. L. Richards during the thirty-one years that he was on the faculty at ASU. One fundamental feature of scientific research collections is their dynamism. The collections aren't repositories of objects, but vouchered data points for the biota and ecology of an area. By incorporating my students' efforts in this research, I continue to document the changing face of plant populations in northeastern Arkansas and contribute to the legacy established by Leon Richards.

The research area of plant taxonomy is no different from any other area in science. When Leon Richards began the collection at ASU in 1963, there was no comprehensive source of information about plants and plant communities in eastern Arkansas. During his career he concentrated on building a resource that reflected the floristic composition of the region and established the baseline for the region. The research holdings continue to be a significant repository of historical floristic and ecological data about the region. By continuing to monitor and track current plant communities and species composition, we can follow changes in plant species assemblages as they occur. We can associate those changes in composition with corresponding changes in land-use patterns. And we can continue to teach successive generations of biologists about the technical identification of plants and the need for a solid understanding of the plants of a region, no matter whether their interest is research or management or as natural history buffs. Part of the education package is the academic and scholarly content of plant biology, and part of it is the always surprising human reactions experienced when people are introduced to the biological and cultural world they inhabit.

Nobody's Dolphins

ALDEMARO ROMERO

🐚 *Venezuela: A Magic Biodiversity Country*—that was the title of a popular book I published in 1993 about the rich variety of species in a country with a wealth of diverse ecosystems. As founder and executive director for eight years of BIOMA, the Venezuelan Foundation for the Conservation of Biodiversity, I was greatly interested in promoting the value of species richness. With a PhD from the Tropical Biology Program at the University of Miami, Florida, and a year and a half of training with the International Program of the Nature Conservancy in Washington, D.C., I had decided to found BIOMA as a not-for-profit organization with the goal of protecting Venezuela's biological resources through scientific research and land acquisition.

Although some Venezuelan fauna had been studied previously, there was a notable exception: the marine mammals. Intending to analyze the conservation status of those animals, I began gathering as much data as possible. One of the people I contacted was Prof. Ignacio Agudo, then an official with the Venezuelan Ministry of the Environment. He provided me with an astonishing amount of unpublished information, the product of his own interest in the subject, which clearly showed a horrifying picture: dolphins in Venezuela were being regularly harpooned in order to use their meat as shark bait. The hooked sharks were then mutilated to harvest their fins, which were exported to the United States and other countries where they had become a favorite delicacy among the "yuppies" of that time.

The story sounded both incredible and tragic, and I was afraid that unpublished documents alone would not move the Venezuelan government to action. So in February 1993, Ignacio and I went to a coastal town

11

Aldemaro Romero with his research boat in Barbados.
PHOTOGRAPH BY JOEL CRESWELL.

Remains of slaughtered dolphins on the beach in Venezuela.
PHOTOGRAPH BY ALDEMARO ROMERO.

in eastern Venezuela whose name kept popping up in reports about dolphin killings: El Morro de Puerto Santo.

We accompanied local fishers and documented their routine dolphin-harpooning operations. They not only freely allowed us to go on board their skiff, but also narrated on camera their dolphin-harpooning technique. They openly discussed the use of the slaughtered dolphins and the number of dolphins they regularly killed. After videotaping and photographing the practice, which was one of the most disgusting things I have ever witnessed, we headed back to Caracas, Venezuela's capital, and thought about what to do with this material. By then, Ignacio, tired of being ignored by the Ministry of the Environment, had left his official post there to found his own private, not-for-profit, conservation organization: Fundacetácea (the Whale Fund).

We decided that engaging in a shouting campaign with the government would accomplish nothing: the fishers would have been imprisoned to calm public opinion and that would have been the extent of the government's involvement. Thus, the best approach—we thought—was to come up with a positive campaign aimed at converting fishers into tourist guides for dolphin watching. By becoming tourist guides, the fishers could make more money and protect the marine mammals at the same time by taking tourists to see the dolphins instead of killing them. In addition, we asked the Venezuelan government to declare the area in which dolphins were routinely killed a marine sanctuary, which would add muscle to our idea. We testified before the Venezuelan Congress and explained our plans to the media and government officials. Yet, nothing happened.

Later, in October 1993, I stopped in Miami during one of my regular trips to the United States to obtain funds for conservation programs in Venezuela and was invited to my alma mater to give a presentation to a Conservation Biology class. I told the story of dolphin killing in Venezuela and showed pictures and portions of the video we had made. On that particular day there was a guest in the class: Russ Rector, the head of a local animal rights group, the Dolphin Freedom Foundation. He said that he had heard of the dolphin killings but had never been able to find evidence of such acts. He asked me if he could have a copy of the video and I agreed; after all, we had already given copies of the video to the Venezuelan government and the media. We also had not copyrighted the video, which, as we learned later the hard way, was a mistake.

Two weeks later I received a call at my office in Caracas from the CNN desk in Miami: they were planning to run a story about the killing of dolphins in Venezuela and wanted to interview me. Thus, in November 1993,

CNN ran the story worldwide. They not only showed portions of the video but also interviewed Venezuelan government officials, one of whom, the Fisheries director, said that those killings had never occurred, that the video was a fake, and that it had probably not even been shot in Venezuela because, among other things, he said one of the fishers was "too fat" to be Venezuelan. Despite these denials, the public reacted intensely to the news: the Venezuelan embassy in Washington and the Venezuelan consulate in Miami claimed to have received more than twenty thousand calls, letters, and faxes of protest from the American public.

As a consequence of this publicity, I began receiving at my home anonymous phone calls, the contents of which ranged from insults to threats in which my daughters' names and school schedules were detailed. Ignacio had similar experiences as well. The reaction from the Venezuelan government was swift: instead of investigating the facts (which we had documented for them in the recent past), they moved to charge Ignacio and myself with "treason to the motherland" for "giving the country a bad name." They arrested the fishers in the video and forced them to "confess" that we had "tricked" them into killing dolphins, despite the fact that one of the fishers on the video told in his own words how frequently they harpooned dolphins.

I knew then that it was safer for me and my family to leave the country, and thus we headed for Miami to stay at Steven Green's house (he had been my PhD adviser at the University of Miami) until I could start a new life. Ignacio, not having the same contacts, went into hiding in Venezuela.

I thought I had left this nightmare behind when, on April 1994, a Venezuelan judge issued a warrant for our arrest and vowed on television that, once arrested, we "would never be released from jail." The news became such a *cause célèbre* that even the *Wall Street Journal* ran a front page story about it in which Ramon Martinez, the governor of Sucre State, where the killings had been documented, was reported as saying, "If it were up to me, I'd have them shot." This was not surprising for a country with a very corrupt justice system and one routinely found to be at fault by human rights organizations as well as the U.S. State Department for their less than stellar human rights records, which include torture, death squads, and *desaparecidos* (the "disappeared" ones). This campaign against us included the editing and mistranslating of our video by agents of anti-environmental groups such as the High North Alliance in order to make it appear that we were ordering the killing of the dolphins. Since we never copyrighted the video, there was nothing we could do to prevent it.

A few weeks later, the Venezuelan government solicited the United States for my extradition; however, the U.S. government knew the circumstances surrounding the request and simply ignored it.

Then, in November 1994, I received a phone call from an Eduardo Vetencourt, who identified himself as the Venezuelan vice-consul in Miami, asking to meet me. I accepted provided we could meet in a public place: the Burger King next to the University of Miami main campus. During a two-hour meeting Vetencourt informed me that he was armed and that his "real job" involved "security." He said that a military plane could pick me up in Miami and take me back to Venezuela, where I would receive a "fair trial." Vetencourt added that the Venezuelan authorities had "temporarily" abandoned the idea of kidnapping me because of fear of bad publicity.

Now that the word "kidnapping" had been used, I informed some friends of mine what Vetencourt had told me, and they contacted the FBI. I explained to the special agents who interviewed me what had happened and the story reached Janet Reno, then U.S. attorney general. According to my contacts, she warned the Venezuelan government that such illegal action would seriously damage U.S.-Venezuelan diplomatic relations and that under international law, were I to be kidnapped and taken to Venezuela, the U.S. government would demand my immediate return.

After that, the Venezuelan government left me alone, and people close to the U.S. government told me that Reno's admonishment had worked.

But, what about Ignacio Agudo?

As I said earlier, Ignacio went into hiding, but his family was harassed. The police would knock on Ignacio's parents' doors every night at midnight, trying to find and arrest him. Ignacio's father, eighty-five years old, committed suicide in June 1994 in order to avoid giving away his son's location, and several government security agents attended his funeral hoping to arrest Ignacio. While he remained in hiding, his young wife, Saida Josefina, who had a heart condition and was not able to get the right medical attention, died in April 1995 at age thirty-six of a heart attack, leaving behind not only Ignacio but also their two daughters, Esther, age five, and Lina, age three months.

Obviously, Ignacio needed to be rescued. I contacted an environmentalist on the island of Aruba, an independent former Dutch possession off the coast of Venezuela, and another in Brazil, Jose Truda Palazzo Jr., to make arrangements for Ignacio to go to that country, where he could receive political asylum. Aruba, which did not require a visa of Venezuelans entering that country, had to be used as a "middle country" for the operation. The question was how to get Ignacio out of Venezuela.

I decided to contact Merritt Clifton, the editor of *Animal People*, a publication dedicated to protecting animals' rights, to ask for his help. Merritt came up with a beautiful idea: he would have someone go to Venezuela on a cruise ship and take advantage of the then weak security measures involving tourists in order to smuggle Ignacio out of the country and deliver him to Aruba.

The people Merritt contacted were Alice and Ken Dodge, who were running a Pet Search no-kill adoption center in their home town of Glencoe, Missouri. The plan required the Dodges to go to Caracas by cruise ship on short notice and at their own expense. Once the dates were set, I phoned Ignacio and made the meeting arrangements. The plan was that Alice would disembark in La Guaira (the nearest port to Caracas) with her husband's boarding pass, pick up Ignacio, and re-embark, pretending that Ignacio was her husband. However, there was a catch: Ignacio did not speak English and Alice did not speak Spanish, so everything had to be carefully planned for the meeting to work. From the beginning the plan went smoothly until Alice and Ignacio were trying to board the cruise ship. Venezuelan guards asked Ignacio to show the stamp with fluorescent ink on his hand, a stamp that he should have received when leaving the ship. Ignacio almost panicked but not Alice; as reported by *Animal People*, "As she approached the checkpoint, returning with Agudo, even people already aboard the ship could hear her tell the world that her 'husband' was a dunce, who would end up with the rats in a Venezuelan jail because he'd moseyed off the ship with his hands in his pockets, and would be lucky if some trigger-happy guard didn't stand him up against a wall and shoot him. The guards didn't like that implication, what they understood of it. They didn't like Alice, a large woman whose rage can terrify even people who are heavily armed. They saw Agudo's discomfort. With a glance of sympathy, they waved him past."

Ignacio spent about a month in Aruba getting his paperwork ready to go to Brazil, where he was received by José Truda. After a letter/fax-writing campaign, Ignacio was officially recognized as a refugee by the United Nations High Commission for Refugees. Yet the Brazilian government, under pressure from Venezuela, almost refused to acknowledge his refugee status, necessitating another public campaign in Brazil to secure his safety.

Brazil denied Ignacio a resident's visa as a political refugee (for the first time in their history), but under international pressure, they agreed to accept him as a regular immigrant. The problem was that he had to get a job to prove himself eligible for immigration, but, of course, he could not get a job without the appropriate papers . . . and he could not obtain those papers without leaving Brazil and re-entering the country, but that would leave him liable to deportation back to Venezuela. At the end and with the help of some local lawyers, the Brazilian government relented and refugee status for Ignacio and his daughters was legalized.

One of the lingering questions in this whole affair is why would Venezuela persecute us with so much intensity and malice when all that we did was expose a well-known problem and propose a solution for it? There are two clues to the answer to this question.

Beginning in 1991, Venezuela had its tuna export to the United States embargoed because its tuna boats that operate in the eastern Pacific Ocean had been killing thousands of dolphins by encircling them with gigantic purse seine nets when pursuing tuna; because in that part of the world it is not unusual for tuna to swim beneath dolphins, fishers encircle dolphins in the hope that tuna will be caught. In fact, part of the smear campaign by the Venezuelan government against Ignacio and me was that we were "paid agents of U.S. tuna companies."

The other clue is even more sinister. After coming to the United States, I learned through both private and public sources that the real reason for the Venezuelan government persecution of us was that many Venezuelan tuna boats had been involved in the smuggling of cocaine to both the United States and Europe. At that time at least, there was a clear connection between drug traffickers and the Venezuelan government to the point that the president of Venezuela pardoned a known drug trafficker. When the affair was revealed, he claimed that it had been an "honest mistake." When Venezuelan tuna boats carrying drugs were captured by U.S. or European authorities, the crews and anyone else involved were prosecuted by those governments, but when the capture occurred in Venezuelan waters, somehow nothing happened. As the then U.S. ambassador in Caracas, Jeffrey Davidow, told my father after I had fled to the United States, "Don't worry about your son; we'll protect him; after all, the enemies of your son are also the enemies of the United States."

More than ten years later one wonders what has happened about all of this. The International Whaling Commission published a report coauthored by Ignacio, Steve Green, and myself about the exploitation of cetaceans in Venezuela. The report was peer-reviewed and was another vindication of our claims that dolphin killing for shark baiting was and had been a common practice in Venezuelan waters for decades. Rights International, a nonprofit and nonpartisan organization that represents victims of human rights violations before international courts, filed a petition in 1996 before the Inter-American Commission of Human Rights in Washington, D.C., on our behalf. The petition sought an injunction against the Venezuelan government and its agents to prohibit the threats of death and kidnapping and other acts committed against Ignacio, myself, and our families; it also sought compensation for damages suffered by us as a consequence of the Venezuelan government's retaliation attempts against us for having released the results of our scientific studies on dolphin mortality. This commission, part of the Organization of American States and notorious for its ineffectiveness and bias toward government positions, refused even to hear the case.

The tuna embargo against Venezuela still stands despite numerous attempts by the Venezuelan government to have it lifted. Venezuela, despite increasing oil revenues, has an unprecedented level of poverty, government corruption, and undemocratic practices, which have been denounced by many international bodies.

Today Ignacio Agudo lives in Brazil with his two daughters and second wife and has become a Brazilian citizen. He continues to work on other areas of natural history. I became a U.S. citizen, reinitiated my academic career, and currently am chair and professor of the Department of Biological Sciences at Arkansas State University, where I teach, among other things, marine mammalogy. My research in the Caribbean continues on marine mammal exploitation, with numerous papers about this issue published in peer-reviewed publications.

As for the dolphins . . . In 1994 an investigative reporter for the American TV show *American Journal* went to Venezuela, to the same town where we had documented dolphin harpooning. One of the fishers in the town had no problem showing in front of the video camera a harpoon head routinely used for killing dolphins and added, "The killing of dolphins continues, just that it is done in secret."

They are still nobody's dolphins.

Additional Readings

Clifton, M. 1996. Artful dodge gets Agudo family out of Venezuela. *Animal People* 5(3): 1, 16.

Romero, A., I. Agudo, and S. Green. 1997. Cetacean exploitation in Venezuela. *Reports of the International Whaling Commission* 47:735–746.

Romero, A., A. I. Agudo, S. M. Green, and G. Notarbartolo di Sciara. 2001. Cetaceans of Venezuela: Their distribution and conservation status. National Oceanographic and Atmospheric Administration Technical Reports. NOAA Technical Report NMFS 151:1–64.

Romero, A., and J. Creswell. 2005. In the land of the mermaid: How culture, not ecology, influenced marine mammal exploitation in the Southeastern Caribbean. In *Environmental issues in Latin America and the Caribbean,* ed. A. Romero and S. West, 3–20. Dordrecht, The Netherlands: Springer.

Safe at last! 1996. *Animal People* 5(5): 16, 22.

Into the Black Water

ALAN CHRISTIAN AND JOHN HARRIS

"IT WAS A DARK and stormy night!" is the feeling experienced by every black-water river diver as he or she begins a descent, at least the ones who survive to become knowledgeable enough to tell the tales. If a diver doesn't have the jitters before a dive, especially a dive at depth, then trouble looms in the darkness. Ah, the darkness! It is so absolute, engulfing, mind-warping, and, well, sometimes terrifying. The descent begins with the "all's well" thumbs up to the dive tender and observers safely planted in the dive boat enjoying the breeze, sunshine, wispy clouds, and the security of a copious air supply.

The adage "You don't know what you're missing until you've been forced to be without it" doesn't do justice to being deprived of air. What is more free than air? Have you ever been without, even just for a minute? Have you ever been forced to be without, to yearn for that next breath, to have lungs and diaphragm that pull from within and receive nothing in return but the burn of deprivation? The panic that can arise from air deprivation can be overwhelming and lethal for the inexperienced diver.

Why Black-Water Dive?

The reason I, Alan Christian, got involved in black-water diving was because government agencies such as the Arkansas Game and Fish Commission, the U.S. Fish and Wildlife Service, and the U.S. Army Corps of Engineers all needed baseline information on the size and composition of mussel beds in the rivers of Arkansas in order to make management decisions concerning endangered and non-endangered species. Since the late 1800s, mussels have been harvested either for the button industry or

21

the cultured pearl industry. For the button industry, freshwater mussel shells have the ideal hard composition for the manufacture of buttons by hole punch through the shell. For the cultured pearl industry, mussel shell particles are the ideal substrate for the production of artificial pearls. Natural pearls are made by oysters when a piece of sand gets between the mantel of the oyster and its shell; to protect itself from the irritation, the oyster secretes mother of pearl over the sand grain, which over time results in a pearl. In the case of artificial pearls, a freshwater-mussel-shell seed is used instead of a grain of sand. To make seeds, the thick shell is cut into cubes, which are then smoothed into sphere-shaped seeds that can be inserted into oysters. This could be a million-dollar industry in Arkansas, if the market demands the shells.

The Dive Rig

The standard dive gear utilized for river diving in the twenty-first century is relatively simple to use and extremely safe when used correctly. It generally consists of a gas-powered generator that drives an oil-less air compressor, which stores air in cylinders or a large-volume tank. All of this equipment must be stationed on a dive platform that is usually just an aluminum johnboat or perhaps a small party barge. Sometimes large-volume air cylinders are brought to the dive site already filled with compressed air, but then these must be refilled at a compression station once the air has been drained. If the boat or barge is equipped with a large-volume tank, the compressed air is delivered to the diver through an air hose, usually fifty to one hundred feet in length. The diver then breathes through a specially adapted "hookah" regulator stuffed in the mouth while the eyes and nose are protected by a dive mask, or air may be drawn by normal breathing into a full face mask or dive helmet adapted for relatively low air pressure.

The dive rig or surface-based air compressor that we use is itself called a "hookah" after the Turkish tobacco-smoking contraption of the same name. The Turkish hookah is basically a fancy tobacco pipe with several long hoses extending from a centralized compartment that allows several people to smoke from the same pipe simultaneously. In the divers' version of the hookah, the main body is an oil-less air compressor powered by a small engine similar to a lawnmower engine; the compressor is connected to the diver by two hoses that supply the diver(s) with air (hence the diver draws air through a regulator) and provide a safety line to the surface. Depending on the model, the hookah will have a reserve tank of some sort that usually provides three to five minutes of back-up air in case such things as your dive buddy forgets to check the gas levels prior to you going down or the rare, but expected, mechanical breakdown occur. In addition to the air hose itself, a safety line, usually a stout nylon or polypropylene rope, is attached to the air hose and allows the diver to return to the surface by hand-over-hand ascent. In case of an emergency, the rope also allows the dive tender to retrieve an incapacitated diver by the same method.

Weight belts or harnesses capable of carrying substantial amounts of lead are worn by divers to assist with their descent and to help anchor them against the current. Wetsuits, dry suits, coveralls, and even plastic rain suits are used by divers to help retain body heat in cold river waters.

The Communications System

In the buddy system used in hookah diving, the dive buddy remains in the boat with the air compressor and carefully monitors the fifty- to one-hundred-foot hoses. Prior to 2001, the only method of communication used by the Arkansas Mussel Survey group consisted of pulling on these hoses, either one, two, or three times. Recently, we began using a two-way communication device on some of our larger river dives, but we still rely primarily on the primitive hose-pulling communication system.

In this system the diver and dive tender communicate with each other by a number of tugs on the air hose. One tug indicates that either the diver or the tender should stop pulling in line or letting out line. Two tugs indicate either that the diver needs more line or that the tender wants to let out more line. Three tugs means either that the diver is in trouble and wants the tender to pull him out of the water or that the tender wants to pull the diver out of the water for some reason. As you can imagine, numerous "discussions" have arisen after "communications" due to differing interpretations of what constitutes one, two, or three tugs. On many occasions a diver has been plucked from the water column unexpectedly because the tender interpreted three tugs when the diver only intended two.

Situations that require the tender to give three tugs are thunderstorms in the area causing dangerous lightning and rain, the engine on the air compressor stopping and the tender not being able to get it started again, and one of the more stressful situations, a barge moving upstream or downstream while the diver is down. When barges approach, we usually only have a few minutes to get the diver up to the surface because mussel beds are typically located in bends of the river that limit one's view both upstream and downstream. Often a barge will be within 450 yards of the diver when it is first sighted!

How It All Started for a Thick-Necked, Weak-Minded Diver

It all started on a mid-summer afternoon in 1991 when I was checking into the Wild River Motel in St. Croix Falls, Wisconsin. I was interning for the Wisconsin Department of Natural Resources (DNR) in the Water Resources Division. My job was collecting point-source effluent from permitted dischargers such as wastewater treatment and industrial facilities. Just after I had finished telling the inn keeper the story of why I was in their quiet river town, a gentleman of distinguished appearance introduced himself as Dr. George Harp of Arkansas State University (ASU). He mentioned that he was an environmental biologist and explained that ASU had a graduate program in biology and environmental science. We exchanged contact information and departed to our respective rooms.

After eating dinner, I decided to take a walk, which was the only entertainment of which I was aware in this small, western, Wisconsin town; I noticed the distinguished-looking professor getting aerial nets out of his trunk. Being an inquisitive undergraduate who had just finished a class in freshwater invertebrates the previous spring, I asked him what he was doing. He replied that he was collecting dawn- and dusk-flying dragonflies that would be skimming the water in about fifteen to thirty minutes as the sun set. Not really having anything else to do, I asked him if I could give him a hand. After a brief moment of silence as he grabbed another net, he handed the net to me and said, "Sure."

We made it down to the river dock just as the dawn and dusk fliers were beginning to nip the surface of the water. Being an enthusiastic student trying to impress the professor, I was determined to collect as many dragonflies with the aerial nets as I possibly could, and I did just that. I caught eight out of the twelve dragonflies that we collected of the species *Neurocordulia yamaskanensi* (Stygian Shadowfly). I was fairly proud of my efforts, and based on Dr. Harp's expressions, he was very happy with the outcome and my ability to collect dragonflies, especially since this was my first time doing so. We slowly walked back to the motel, and after exchanging our satisfaction with the catch and some pleasantries, we both went into our respective rooms. I awoke the next day and went about my business collecting effluent from the St. Croix Falls wastewater treatment plant, not really thinking much about the events of the previous day.

So, you may ask, what does this have to do with black-water diving? Well, about a month and a half later, I was sitting in the office at the Wisconsin DNR doing paperwork when I received a call from Dr. Harp asking me if I was interested in an assistantship doing mussel surveys in Arkansas that would be available for the fall semester, which was only three weeks away. I explained to him that I still had one semester left at the University of Wisconsin at Oshkosh and that I was playing semi-pro football that fall and coaching the running backs at the university, but I would be interested in attending in the spring. So I made a visit to Arkansas State University in November of 1991 and decided to begin classes and my assistantship diving for mussels in January.

Nothing unexpected or traumatic happened until late May of 1992. I had completed a semester of graduate school and gotten scuba trained in a swimming pool and certified in the crystal-clear springs of Florida over spring break. The first week in the field, the two graduate students who were training me decided to break me in easy and have me do boat work for the first part of the week while they did the diving. The waters of the lower Black River in late May, after the spring rainy season, tend to have a reddish-brown hue, resembling that of chocolate milk. Their decision to keep me in the boat for the first part of the week, while probably made with good intentions, only gave my imagination time to brew up images of killer alligator snappers and enormous flathead catfish. This leads into my first full dive experience.

John Harris was my experienced trainer; John is known among divers as "Big Daddy" and is famous for the stories he tells around the beer keg at old diver meetings. One of Big Daddy's more entertaining and often-told stories at these diver rendezvous is the one about me, affectionately known as the strapping lad, thick of neck and weak of mind, just the way you like a good black-water diver equipped.

Against Big Daddy's better judgment, I started my career in black water at a depth of fourteen feet. The current was gentle, but the darkness complete, as I began my descent. The older diver, now relegated to boat tender, could only watch as the bubbles from my fear-induced, quickened breaths rose in a near continuous stream to the surface. Five minutes, ten minutes, fifteen minutes—Big Daddy was impressed that I was certainly giving this first dive the full treatment. He thought that I must have found something extremely interesting because I remained in one spot for several minutes. Five more minutes passed, and Big Daddy saw no movement, but

Alan Christian in boat, preparing to dive.
PHOTOGRAPH BY MITCH WINE.

plenty of bubbles rising to the surface. The older diver was pleased that I had taken so easily and completely to the daunting environment below, and then without notice, it started.

Thousands of tiny bubbles began to break the surface of the river, and then slowly, agonizingly, a sliver of tree branch broke the surface. And then inch by inch, another sliver, and then a whole limb, and then the trunk of a good-sized tree rose from the depths, and attached securely to this massive anchor was I, frantically treading water, air hose and safety rope hopelessly wrapped round and round and round the tree trunk. Then, speaking with the air-supply regulator clinched firmly between my teeth, I hissed as best I could in staccato syllables, "I—don't—think—I—can—do—this—much—longer."

To which Big Daddy leaned over and replied, "Drop your weight belt." You see, the weight-belt harness in use had quick-release levers designed for just this situation, and all I had to do was pop three levers, and I was free to surface. My thick neck, weak mind, and I, along with my arboreal companion, immediately re-descended; the trunk, limbs, and slivers all disappeared to the depths much more quickly than they had surfaced, and a few seconds later I bobbed to the surface as if shot from a water cannon. Big Daddy said that, to my credit, this episode did not deter my diving career, and I have carved quite a nice career niche for myself from this inauspicious beginning. Fortunately, my neck was thick enough (remember the football experience) to enable me to pull the entire tree to the surface with me, but my mind was not so weak that I have ever needed that lesson again.

Training to Survive

Training a black-water river diver usually starts with a practice session in a shallow, relatively clear river to enable the novice to gain experience with the equipment and nuances of the current, look at the pretty fish, and become one with the aquatic environment without the heart-pounding fear associated with total darkness. Even at that, river diving can be a harrowing experience. Once, another young trainee of Big Daddy (John Harris) was experiencing his very first river dive, and as luck would have it, a kink developed in the dive hose, totally blocking his air supply. The young man sucked and pulled on the regulator for air to no avail; he frantically paddled to the surface and yelled for assistance. The two trainers, one being Big Daddy, remained sitting nonchalantly in the boat, not lifting a finger to help; the young diver was fully extended some one hundred feet away from presumed safety and, in his mind, mere seconds from death. A second Herculean effort raised the young man's head to the surface once again, eyes big as saucers, and he once again yelped, "HELP!"

At this time the older, more experienced trainer rose to his feet, stood on the bow of the boat, and shouted, "Stand Up!" For you see, the young diver was in barely six feet of water, and had he not panicked, he could have merely stood up and put his head above the water for air. And the most important lesson for divers was learned at little cost: panic will kill you deader than a doorknob when diving. A cool head will get you out of almost every situation; a panic attack will turn you into a floater when death is easily avoidable.

John Harris in full dive gear preparing to enter the water.
PHOTOGRAPH BY JOSH SEAGRAVES.

Bringing in a Diver: Treetops, Boat Bottoms, and Graceful Entrances

One of the more interesting parts of black-water diving is bringing a diver back to and into the boat. Some divers like to pull themselves back to the boat while others prefer for the dive tender to do the pulling. When a diver prefers to be pulled back to the boat by the tender, a situation often arises that can put the diver in a precarious position. For example, neither the tender nor the diver knows what obstructions are between the diver and the boat, so a well-intentioned dive tender may pull a diver into or through a treetop. This puts the diver in an alarmed state of mind to say the least. It is also somewhat confusing to the dive tender when he or she doesn't understand why the diver cannot be pulled out of the water when there seems to be plenty of line remaining in the water! The diver, on the other hand, knows exactly what is going on, as he or she is being pinned next to the large obstruction; and the harder the dive tender pulls, the closer the diver comes to this obstruction and sometimes the less air the diver receives due to pinched hoses.

Even when the path to the boat is clear, there are still hazards that divers may face that are beyond their control. Many divers have been pulled swiftly through the water expecting to have a clear path to the surface only to meet the bottom of the boat with their heads. The first clue to the dive tender that this has happened is the loud thump originating from the bottom of the boat, and second clue is the angry or star-gazed look of the diver as he enters the boat.

However, even if a diver makes it to the surface unharmed by his dive tender, the last step of the return into the boat can also be a dangerous and humorous one. Any vision of a diver climbing the ladder and gracefully stepping into the boat must be prefaced by the fact that large-river divers typically need to wear fifty or so extra pounds of weight, either distributed along a weight belt around the waist or distributed on a harness worn across the torso of the diver. As you can imagine, wearing a weight harness causes the diver to be a bit "top heavy." While ideal for equally distributing the weight and for keeping a diver on the bottom of the river in swift currents, the weight harness does make for some interesting entrances into the boat. While attempting to enter the boat, many divers end up swinging back and forth on the ladder due to their high centers of mass, imitating those fluid-filled feeding-bird knickknacks that dip their heads into and out of the bird feeder. Once the diver gracefully accomplishes that climb on the ladder, he or she is not out of the woods yet, as the step into the boat can be quite challenging. Some divers manage it stylishly by throwing one leg at a time into the boat; others do a not-so-graceful roll, while others just fall head first into the boat.

On one occasion after a long day's work with fifty or so pounds of weight on my torso, I was having issues with the ladder and my weight distribution; in fact, I resembled that feeding bird, teeter tottering back and forth until, finally, I fell forward into the boat. The fall, while graceful, was right into the dive flag attached to the air compressor. I hit the dive flag with my shoulder and snapped the flag in two. The sound of that snap was as loud as a gunshot and caused my dive tender, who was turned around taking care of some gear, to quickly turn around, only to see me face down on the bottom of the boat, lying flat and motionless while I was trying to determine just what had happened to me. In fact, he joked afterward that he though I had been shot by someone as I entered the boat.

Welcome to the White

In 1992 I made my first dive in the White River, and by this time I thought I was an experienced diver. The White River of Arkansas and Missouri is famous for many reasons, such as its trophy trout that can be caught in the river below the big lakes of Arkansas and Missouri, the destruction of the USS *Mound City* by Union gunboats on the White River in Arkansas at the battle of Saint Charles during the Civil War, and the mid-nineteenth-century steamboats that made regular runs between White River ports and the larger cities of Memphis and New Orleans, capturing the essence of comfort and elegance and often sinking with passengers and crew aboard. However, for a diver, a river of this size has its own mystique; but at first glance, its waters appeared deceptively gentle. At the surface, the water did not seem to be moving very fast, and I didn't imagine that it was very deep; of course, the river was muddy and I couldn't see the bottom. I expected this to be a pretty uneventful dive.

However, once I entered the water, I quickly realized that I was entering the domain of a fierce and unrelenting beast. It was at this point that I realized that I was no longer in control, but in the hands of the mighty White River. As I climbed my way down the anchor line, I felt like a flag on a flag pole in a hurricane. As I tightly gripped the anchor line, the current stretched my body parallel to the bottom of the river. Fortunately, I had on enough weight that eventually I made it to the bottom of the line; but after five minutes of pulling myself hand over hand down the line, I was huffing and puffing on my regulator when I got to the bottom. Mussel beds in the White River are typically at depths of thirty to forty-five feet. I took a minute to catch my breath and bring my heart rate down before I made my next move.

My next step after leaving the anchor line was to place my hands and feet on the river bottom and lie flat on my belly to help reduce drag. This is what I had done in every other river in which I had dived in Arkansas, but I quickly realized that the White River was not like any of the other rivers. In the White River, when I placed my hands and feet down in the sand, the swiftly moving water instantly scoured out the sand around them. The sand and water were moving so fast that it felt as though the bottom of the river was vibrating; my hands and feet tingled as though being massaged by an electric vibrator. It was not at all what I had imagined at the surface.

The lower White River receives cold water released from the dams holding the big lakes in the upper and middle sections of the state. Therefore, in addition to the rapidly moving water pounding your body, this cold water chills a diver to the bones, even on the hottest August days in Arkansas. It might be 100 degrees in the boat, but I have come from the bottom of the White in a full wetsuit after only an hour in the water, chilled to the bone and covered with goose bumps. You can just imagine how long it takes to warm up after a dive in late October or in early winter!

But the White River is not finished until a diver is back in the boat. After collecting mussels, a diver still has to make it back to the top. The ascent is always a workout and a challenge to any White River diver. The descent is hard enough, the ferocious water velocity, the cold, but then the diver has to climb up a rope or dive hose lugging a bag full of mussels, sometimes with over 150 individuals, from depths of thirty to forty-five feet. So an already-tired diver begins the ascent, fighting the unrelenting current, which now has a larger surface area on which to pound—diver and bag of mussels. I always hope that the anchors hold and that I don't have to climb through tree limbs to finally get to the surface. Needless to say, I always sleep well after a day of diving on the White River.

"Jump In": The Training Techniques of an Old-School Clarendon Sheller

In July of 1993 I had finished all but the last few miles of the survey of the Cache River, and it was not quite time for us to go back to the White River, as August is typically when water levels drop enough to allow for safer and more efficient diving. The autumn before, I had started surveying the

White River at Newport, working my way down to the mouth, a trek of over two hundred river miles. I needed to get more mussel-bed information from that region, so Big Daddy suggested that I call one of the most experienced shellers (people who dive for mussels and sell the shells to the cultured pearl industry) and ask if he would be willing to run the river with me for two or three days while the river was still up and I had some time. So I did.

Most people are not familiar with shellers, but they typically are an eccentric group, mostly mavericks of sorts that have colorful backgrounds and live a simple life. When I called this gentleman in Clarendon and arranged the three-day visit, he insisted that I stay at his place because he said there was no place in town fit for a visitor. Even though I was somewhat skeptical, I was young and needed his help, so I felt I couldn't turn down his invitation. I figured that would offend him and he might not take me on the river, so I reluctantly agreed to stay with him. I could not have imagined what was about to happen to me.

I arrived at his place the night before we were scheduled to dive; I was greeted by a gentleman whose voice reminded me of Johnny Cash, and I got the distinct impression that he had the same rustic nature that Johnny Cash portrayed. When I reflect on this incident, I realize that my impressions were correct. As I entered the house on a late July evening, the first thing I noticed, being a newly initiated southerner originating from Wisconsin, was that this gentleman's house did not have air-conditioning. That was another sign that this was going to be an interesting visit since I sweat in Arkansas as soon as the temperature hits about 70 degrees in April and don't stop till late September! As expected, I slept very little that night, but I tried to remember that he was doing me a favor. As I walked into the kitchen that next morning, the eccentric sheller greeted me with a glass of hot coffee; yes, I said it right, a glass of hot coffee. This is when I started really thinking, "What have I gotten myself into?" and "Wait until I see Big Daddy; he is going to pay for setting me up with this fellow."

Before we went to the river, he wanted to show me some of the artwork and crafts that he and his wife made in their spare time with mussel shells and gar scales. Gar scales are typically large and, when dried, look like Indian spear heads. Among the various craft pieces that he showed me were soap dishes made out of mussel shells and tie pins made out of mussel shells that were carved into spears and put on the head of the pin. One of the more creative and interesting designs that he showed me, and one that still amazes me today, was his Christmas tree carefully

constructed of gar scales! Remember, I was still a young and fairly sheltered kid from Wisconsin; I had never before been exposed to a character
such as the Clarendon sheller.

The first two days on the river went fairly well and the sheller really
taught me a lot about identifying where mussel beds are on the White by
reading the river and the riverbank. His lessons were invaluable and I was
learning a lot, and I had really become comfortable with this gentleman.
However, I was getting the impression that while he thought I had gained
some good experience working on the Cache River, he felt that I was still
a greenhorn on the White. So on the third morning at breakfast with my
glass of hot coffee, he announced to me that we were going to do some
diving. I was a bit concerned about this since I had not brought any of my
dive gear such as my bathing suit, wetsuit, mask, dive booties, etc. When
I told him that I did not have any dive gear with me, he just looked me
over and said, "You are about my size; I will let you use some of my
stuff." Again, a bit skeptical and sheltered, I anxiously agreed.

He left me for a few minutes to look for the dive gear. He came back
with an old pair of boots, a pair of polyester pants, and a cotton button-
up shirt. He handed them to me and said, "Put these on." As you might
expect, I was a bit confused; these items were not part of the dive gear
that I normally used, but I convinced myself that these must be the under-
garments he was providing me.

Well, we got to the boat and motored upstream to the mouth of the
Cache, just upstream of Clarendon. We boated up into the Cache a bit; at
which point the old sheller, dressed similarly to me, exclaimed to me that
he was going to dive the Cache and show me where to find mussels in
this lower stretch of river. So, as I was in the boat preparing to be his dive
tender, expecting to be as thorough as I had been taught and going
through the systematic buddy-system checklist described above, he started
up the hookah, put on his weight belt, put on his full face mask attached
to the air hose, grabbed a collection bag, and immediately jumped overboard straight into the water in a free descent. As this happened, I was
somewhat in shock, first, because he dove in without a dive suit and, second, because he did a free descent without the anchor line, the psycholog-
ical safety net that I was accustomed to using. After a few minutes, he
pulled himself back to the boat using the air hose and climbed back into
the boat. His bag was filled with mussels. As he dumped them out, he
provided me with a detailed description of where the mussels were in the
stream. I was still in shock over the cavalier attitude he had exhibited on
the dive. After testing me on my mussel identification, he then instructed

me to get the gear ready and told me that we were going back to the White, where it would be my turn to dive to find White River mussels. I was still in shock and now had heightened anxiety, as I was not sure that I could be as cavalier as he was.

As we approached the mussel bed at Clarendon, I became even more apprehensive because the White River water level was still a bit above the level that Big Daddy had suggested. Nevertheless, because I liked to think of myself as being a macho football player and because I was determined to show that I was worthy of being called a mussel diver even in my polyester pants, boots, and button-up shirt, I put on my weight belt and the full face mask and prepared to go in the water. As I started to get in the water, he handed me a collection bag, gave me some last-minute instructions on where the mussels were, and said, "Jump in," and I did.

I fell straight down twenty-one feet into the ferocious White River. The river graciously accepted me in my free fall, but the whole time I was thinking that I was such a goofball for doing this and that I was going to really let Big Daddy have it for sending me here. Then I noticed the cold. A complete chill ran across my body, and I realized, oh, that is why we wear full dive suits in the White, because it is cold, really cold without them. Regardless, I had a point to prove, so after I righted myself on the bottom and caught my breath, I began to move slowly across the bottom in search of mussels. It wasn't long before I found myself on top of mussels and hurriedly began collecting them and putting them in my bag. I filled the bag and immediately began to pull myself up to the surface; I realized that I was chilled to the bone. Once back in the boat, it was 95 degrees, but I still had chill bumps as I emptied my bag. I got the feeling, however, that I had convinced the old-school sheller that I might be okay after all. As I stated before, I learned a lot those three days from the Clarendon sheller. I never saw him again after that day, but each time that I pull up to the Clarendon boat ramp, I think of the old-school sheller and all I learned from him.

Search for Treasures at Preston's Ferry

I learned a valuable lesson about staying on task during a weekend dive while collecting data for my master's thesis on the lower White River. My dive buddy and I were at the Preston's Ferry quadrant sampling a mussel bed. While I was down collecting mussels out of a quad, a colorful local resident pulled up to our boat and began talking to my dive tender. When

I came up, the man asked me if I wanted to make several hundred dollars by looking for his boat that had sunk there the previous weekend. I knew that I needed to be sampling because I was not going to finish this project on time if I didn't use every opportunity I had, but I was also a starving graduate student.

I agreed to stop sampling and take a look for his boat. Well, the water depth at Preston's Ferry averages about thirty-five feet, and while it was reasonably clean on the bottom that day, there were treetops in the bed that we knew about, and the current was moderately swift. At the beginning of my search for this boat, I moved fairly slowly and cautiously, making sure not to make a mistake. But after about fifteen to twenty minutes, I started second guessing myself about my decision. First, was it legal for me to make money while I using the university's boat? Second, as time was going by, I kept thinking that this was keeping me away from what I really needed to be doing, which was sampling. So I became hasty; I moved quickly and carelessly, trying to cover ground, hoping to find the boat, make my money, and get back to sampling, when all of a sudden, my air supply stopped. At first I thought the problem might be at the surface, so I stopped moving and my air restarted. However, when I started moving again, the air stopped again. So I stepped backwards, and my air was fine again. I moved to the left, but no air, so I moved back. Then I moved to the right, but no air, so I moved back. Then I moved backwards again, but again no air, so I moved back. As you can see, I was in a predicament; when I moved in any direction, I was cut off from my air supply.

Being well familiar with our line-pulling signals, I decided that I would just pull my line for help. When I did that, it also temporarily cut off my air supply; that was okay because I immediately got it back, but there was no reply from my dive buddy! I tried that several times to no avail. What was I going to do now?

After several minutes, I decided that my only option was to drop my weight belt and swim to the surface. However, because I was in complete darkness, I had no idea what lay ahead of me. I reasoned that the hose might be caught on something, probably a treetop. Was I in the middle of a tree? What was I caught on? In addition to that, it was at least thirty-five feet to the surface; did I have enough air for the ascent, especially with the current also carrying me downstream, and the velocity there was pretty fast.

Fortunately, I was wearing a wetsuit that caused me to be buoyant; at least I knew I would float up. I contemplated this for a bit, and then got the courage to do it. I took one more gulp of air, dropped my weight belt, and pushed off of the bottom to propel myself into the water column. I followed my dive line for most of the way up until I ran into the problem; a large treetop had somehow grabbed and entangled my air hose.

I pulled my way through the treetop and darted to the water's surface. I popped up near the dive boat. My ascent to the surface was a complete surprise to my dive tender; his eyes were as big as saucers when he saw me. I quickly swam to the boat and caught my breath. Eventually, we were able to recover both the dive hose and the weight belt without getting into the water, but it did take some struggling. That was about as close to death as I have ever come. The moral of the story to me was, "Don't get greedy and stay on task or something will kill you."

The Cache River Glow

Of all of the black-water rivers in which I have dived, the Cache stands out to me as offering the most unique continuum of different colors of light evolving to complete darkness as one descends through the ever-murkier water. The Cache River carries a significant load of sand, silt, and clay throughout the year, and I have never really seen it "clear," but the descent into the depths and ascent back to the surface of this river are different to me.

First, unlike most other rivers, light is reflected and absorbed at the surface, surrounding a diver in a bright yellow haze in which one can make out objects in the water at close distances (say an arm's length), but there is no way to see out of the water, say, into the boat. As one goes a bit deeper, the haze changes from bright yellow to yellowish-red where one can still see light, but instead of seeing objects themselves in the water, one sees what looks like a shadow or outline. The next level is the gray zone; there is still some light, but one only sees a shadow or outline at close distances and then not very well. A diver is surrounded by an eerie semi-dark aura. The fourth and final zone is the pitch black, where everything is completely dark, as if one is in a closet with no light shining under the door. The descent can be a very peaceful and surreal time for a diver; the continuum from partial light to dark allows a diver a few moments to adjust to the surroundings. The ascent is as I would imagine a newborn's arrival to the external world, as one is thrust out of the darkness to the bright sunlight that pierces unadjusted eyes.

John Harris and Alan Christian prepare to dive
the Cache River in March 2007.
PHOTOGRAPH BY MITCH WINE.

An Eye-Opening Start

Another memorable black-water dive with which I was associated was
one with a new recruit from southern Arkansas who had just finished his
undergraduate work a few weeks earlier and was going to be the next
graduate student on the Arkansas Mussel Project of the 1990s. He was
also newly dive certified and had only enjoyed the clear type of diving that
most of us more experienced black-water divers try to avoid, mostly
because easy clear-water diving would probably make us not want to go
back to black-water diving. He had joined us on the lower Cache River for
a few days and learned the ropes of the dive tender prior to the day of his
first dive. He understood how we went about things and we were all feeling pretty confident.

So that afternoon we decided that it was time for him to enter the water and give it a shot. He put on his dive gear and we went through all of the pre-dive checks; I could see that he was neither over nor under confident in this endeavor, but just taking it all matter-of-factly. As I am with all new divers, I was very attentive and gave him instruction on how to proceed and assured him that I would be right there in the boat holding the dive hose. After listening to my last-minute instructions and assurance, he slowly crawled down the ladder and began to go under water. I watched him as his head went under water, but after only about five seconds, he appeared back on the surface. He was breathing heavily; he took out his mouthpiece and exclaimed, "It's dark down there!"

At this point, afraid that he was going to decide that this was not for him, I smiled and in my most compassionate voice said, "Yep." He asked for a minute to catch his breath, which he did, and went back down. He tells the story slightly differently. He remembers that I put my foot on his head and said, "Get back down and don't come up until you find some mussels!" I'm sure that's not the way it happened.

He was down for about five minutes after that, but I am pretty sure that he never moved from the spot where he landed and never let go of the anchor safety line. Regardless, he did become an excellent dive buddy that summer on the Cache River and an excellent black-water diver in general. However, he does admit to not liking to dive the mighty White. As an aside, his self-proclaimed nickname back in those days was his initials followed by MD, for "mussel diver," not medical doctor!

Ode to the White

The last thing I did as I finished that first survey of the lower White River, and that I now do at the end of any project that I do on the White, was thank her for allowing me to work within her confines over those few years. In my mind, I made it out alive because she allowed me to escape. I still have a great respect for that river, and I appreciate what she has allowed me to do. Divers stay alive on the White by not forgetting that she can be a violent and raging competitor.

The Bronze Adonis

Another young diver of Big Daddy's, dubbed the bronze Adonis for his deep, rich tan, long flowing locks, and muscular physique, was quite casual regarding diving at greater depths, in fast flows, and in dark conditions. In short, he was a natural. Seldom did he wear a dive hood to protect his head from obstructions, preferring instead to feel his long locks blowing, if you will, in the aquatic breeze. Sometimes he forgot to strap on his dive knife, the only piece of equipment generally carried to fend off the demons of the depths, monstrous snapping turtles, carnivorous fishes, and other real or imagined dangers. Truly, the most serious threat to diver safety in river waters is the myriad of fishing tackle that lurks below—gill nets, hoop nets, trammel nets, and trot lines—all just as willing to snag a diver as a large fish.

On this day, while Big Daddy served as the dive tender, bronze Adonis was at a depth of about twenty-five feet, enjoying the current as it roiled around him, when he realized he was securely snagged by a stout hook through and through the safety rope. Adonis was not one to abandon the rig, so he groped around the gravelly bottom and found a sharp mussel shell of the heel-splitter variety and began to saw away at the line attached to the hook. Thirty minutes later Adonis triumphantly broke the surface, hook still through his safety line, and marveled at his ingenuity in the face of almost certain death, well, maybe possible death, well, if the air had run out, he would have had to drop the weight belt and free ascend to the surface. But still Adonis thought it was a pretty neat trick, even though he knew that it was dumb to forget his dive knife, which he seldom if ever did again.

The Monster

The older diver, known in his younger years as "Big Daddy," but in his later years as "Pops," was not without tales of mystery and intrigue or at least fear and loathing on the river bottom. Pops had an experience with a monster of the deep that left him wondering if his heart beat would ever return below 120. Pops descended on a forty-foot river dive with the bottom pitch black and the current velocity so fast that the substrate literally quaked as if alive. When the old guy finally got down, he dug in with all fours and grunted frequently, as if that actually helped him stay glued to the bottom. After a meager exploration, moving carefully a few feet one way and then the other, Pops literally fell into a four-foot-deep trench. When Pops fell, he landed smack dab on top of something alive, something big and slimy, and apparently Pops scared it as badly as it scared Pops! After a monumental struggle for what seemed like forever, but was probably only seconds, the two combatants separated to their respective habitats and inspected the damage. All Pops could really do was lie face down in the river mud, pray his heart didn't explode, and hope he hadn't soiled his wetsuit. Upon later examination, Pops was proud to exclaim that he had not lost control of his bodily functions.

The Alligator

Pops had another near-death experience, this time involving something that was clearly under his control. While Pops and a group of younger divers were preparing for a dive down south, one of the boat tenders noted that a log was floating down river against the far bank and expressed the sentiment that care should be taken. Upon further review, Pops came to the realization that the log was, in fact, one *Alligator mississippiensis*, and a nice, healthy specimen at that. Not only did the alligator keep coming downstream to the dive area, it had the audacity to park its potential-handbag body right across from the boat and stare and then slowly, very, very slowly sink out of site.

Now Pops had a situation. He could abort the dive, and truly nobody would have blamed him. But then, for the rest of the day, every other dive could have potentially held the same danger and the same excuse could have been made to abort all the dives. And the next time divers gathered for drunken revelry, Pops would be sure to hear the occasional cluck, cluck, cluck chicken call. And even though he often protested greatly to the contrary, Pops secretly fancied himself a macho pioneering explorer of the riverine environment, but not like the sophisticated Frenchman Jacques Cousteau. Pops liked to proclaim himself as more like Jim Bridger, a trapper, explorer, and mountain man of the 1800s who opened up the Rocky Mountains to the first white settlers and was the first white man to see the Great Salt Lake. So he had to dive with the gator, and dive he did.

Now once he got out of sight from the surface, Pops rolled up into a tight ball and spent about ten minutes rolling around on the bottom, putting on a good show, and praying that the time for him to pay for his voluminous sins had not arrived. He just couldn't imagine a worse fate than being gnawed by a big gator. Fortunately for Pops, the gator was a no-show, but Pops tells the tale often and finds every excuse under the sun to never again go back down south.

Mardi Gras Hallucinations

Black-water diving is not all thrills and chills; it can be downright hallucinogenic. Once Pops was diving in a particularly deep, swift hole and was down on the bottom exploring with his air hose fully extended. It had to be fifty-five or sixty feet deep and the pressure from the fast moving water and depth was really noticeable, verging on uncomfortable. Pops was exploring and found a steeply descending bank that went into an even-deeper abyss that was beckoning, yet foreboding. Pops wanted to push the limits, but at the same time was reluctant to do so.

And then it happened; the steady, strong pressure on the air-hose and safety-line combo lifted Pops from the security of the sandy bottom into the blackness of space, the emptiness of the abyss. The anchors had dragged free from the sand, the boat had drifted downstream, and the safety line had pulled Pops into the void. He first panicked, but then became strangely calm, floating suspended from the line and staring into the blackness. The only sensation was water flowing through the exposed hairs on his hands, making each hair seem independent and responsible for reporting its own actions. The light show began shortly thereafter with explosions of color and white light seemingly emanating from within the mask covering his eyes, but certainly more accurately, it was ratcheting from the depths of his sensory-deprived brain. It was better than fireworks on the Fourth of July.

Serenity in the Dark

Diving in black-water conditions, as you may have gathered by now, involves some ability to cope with the loss of sight in addition to the relative loss of hearing and speaking that is typically associated with diving. This loss of sight can be frightening to beginning black-water divers; however, after divers gain some experience, diving without sight can become quite peaceful and spiritual. In complete or nearly complete darkness and with very little noise other than the diver's own breathing and humming or the occasional drum (a big ugly-looking fish) call, a diver may become absorbed in his or her own thoughts and be able to think about things uninterrupted as at no other time. Once a diver becomes comfortable engulfed in the darkness with only the sense of touch, the mind and the imagination are free to roam and explore and create. This can, however, lull one into a false sense of security until a catfish is disturbed or a snapping turtle is grabbed by mistake.

Additional Readings

Christian, A. D., C. L. Davidson, W.R.I. Posey, P. J. Rust, J. L. Farris, J. L. Harris, and G. L. Harp. 2000. Growth curves of four species of commercially valuable freshwater mussels (Bivalvia: Unionidae) in Arkansas. *Journal of the Arkansas Academy of Sciences* 54:41–50.

Christian, A. D., and J. L. Harris. 2005. Development and assessment of a large blackwater stream sampling design for freshwater mussel assemblages in the lower Cache River, Arkansas. *American Midland Naturalist* 153:90–99.

Christian, A. D., J. L. Harris, W.R.I. Posey, J. F. Hockmuth, and G. L. Harp. 2005. Freshwater mussel (Mollusca: Unionidae) assemblages of the lower Cache River, Arkansas. *Southeastern Naturalist* 4:487–512.

Harris, J. L., and M. E. Gordon. Undated. *Arkansas Mussels.* Little Rock, AR: Arkansas Game and Fish Commission.

———. 1987. Distribution and status of rare and endangered mussels (Mollusca: Margaritiferidae, Unionidae) in Arkansas. *Proceedings Arkansas Academy of Science* 41:49–55.

Harris, J. L., P. J. Rust, S. W. Chordas III, and G. L. Harp. 1993. Distribution and population structure of freshwater mussels (Unionidae) in Lake Chicot, Arkansas. *Proceedings of the Arkansas Academy of Science* 47:38–43.

Harris, J. L., P. J. Rust, A. D. Christian, W. R. Posey II., C. L. Davidson, and G. L. Harp. 1997. Revised status of rare and endangered Unionacea (Mollusca: Margaritiferidae, Unionidae) in Arkansas. *Journal of the Arkansas Academy of Science* 51:66–89.

Face to Face and Nose to Shoulder

THOMAS RISCH

❧ AS AN ANIMAL ECOLOGIST, I study free-ranging populations of wild animals. Since I'm particularly interested in questions relating to reproductive success, I work with large numbers of tagged animals that I can recapture during their lifetimes. Thus, I spend a lot of time handling these animals and collecting a great deal of data from each individual. Although most of my study species are not dangerous, I am in the field a great deal, which puts me in close contact with all sorts of critters, and some of these can make field work somewhat of a hair-raising experience.

My PhD research focused on questions about family size or litter size. To address these, I studied the southern flying squirrel at the Savannah River Ecology Laboratory (SREL) in South Carolina near the Georgia border. Many people don't realized that flying squirrels are very abundant and common throughout the eastern United States. They require forests of oak and hickory that provide an abundance of their favorite food—nuts. The SREL is located on a large Department of Energy facility, the Savannah River Site (SRS) that has plenty of mature nut-producing trees and an abundance of southern flying squirrels. Of course, being a large tract of public-restricted land, the SRS is full of an abundance of wildlife and is a very important refuge for all sorts of migratory birds, wild turkey, fox, amphibians, reptiles, and coyote, just to name a few.

Catching flying squirrels for data collection involves putting nest boxes about fifteen feet high in trees. The squirrels use these boxes just as they do tree cavities. Flying squirrels are almost strictly nocturnal, so I checked boxes during the day to catch the squirrels while they were

One of the flying squirrel houses and
tree-climbing belts used by Thomas Risch.
PHOTOGRAPH BY JOY TRAUTH.

sleeping. I had over one thousand of these boxes on the SRS, so I spent the better part of the daylight hours moving from box to box, climbing up to the boxes on a ten-foot ladder. By the time my PhD work was completed, I had spent over five years in the woods carrying around a ten-foot ladder studying flying squirrels.

When I came to an occupied box, it might contain anywhere from one to ten squirrels. Since I was studying reproduction, I was most interested in finding a box with a female and her pups. By marking the pups, I could assess their survival and growth and relate those data back to the mother. I was able to collect data from over 450 litters of flying squirrel pups, but a single nest-box check stands out.

It was a cool winter's day when I came across this particular box full of squirrels. When I peeked in the box, it was clear that there was a family inside, as I could see the large female with her nearly grow pups. As I always did when I discovered a box with squirrels, I unhooked the box and brought it to the ground; there I removed the squirrels from the box one by one. In order to reduce squirrel stress while they are being handled and marked, each squirrel is lightly drugged during this process by placing it in a plastic container with a small amount of the drug Metaphane soaked onto a cotton ball. The squirrels quickly go into a sleeplike state when exposed to Metaphane. I also stuff a rag into the opening of the nest box to prevent the squirrels remaining in the box from escaping before it is their turn to be marked and measured.

Each squirrel gets two types of tags, an ear tag in each ear and a microchip that is injected under the skin. I also mass each one and take a variety of measurements. These measurements include the length and width of the head and the lengths of the body, tail, a back leg, and a front leg. It takes about ten minutes per squirrel if they need to be tagged, so when I have a box full of squirrels, it can take quite some time to process all of them. After all the squirrels in a nest box have been tagged, measured, and returned to their box, the box is returned to the tree, where the squirrels seem to drift right back asleep.

When I got this particular box to the ground, I was excited to see that it contained a very large litter of five pups. Neither the mother nor her juvenile offspring had been tagged, so I began the procedure of tagging and data collection described above, knowing that it might take me an hour to complete. As I sat on the ground with my legs crossed, collecting data, I heard an unfamiliar noise. It was an animal or group of animals moving through the woods. I'd heard animals moving through the woods almost every day during this research, but I couldn't identify this sound because it sounded too loud and carefree. As I worked on the squirrels, I pondered the sound in my thoughts. "It can't be deer; they'd only make such a racket if they were being chased by something; besides this sound was fairly slow and deliberate. No way is it a fox or raccoon since these animals barely make a sound when they move."

I started wondering if it could be a small pack of wild dogs that are known to inhabit the SRS. These medium-sized dogs, know as Carolina dogs, are also called "American dingoes" since they are adapted to a feral existence and resemble the wild dingoes of Australia. I had a particular interest in these dogs and was doing some research with my colleagues at the SREL on their behaviors. However, our work was done with captive dogs, and I had rarely been able to watch them in the wild.

These thoughts were occupying my mind for almost thirty minutes as I quickly worked through the data collection and marking of the squirrels. When I finished each drugged squirrel, I placed it next to the box since the box still contained wide-awake squirrels that were trying frantically to pull out the rag from the entrance hole and make their escape. I also had to be attentive to the drugged squirrels that I had already measured to make sure that none of them awoke and ran away. So although the sound of this animal or pack of animals was in my thoughts, it was only in the back of my mind as I had plenty to keep me occupied. That is until I realized that this noise was coming down the narrow foot trail that had been worn from my years of nest-box checking and was, in fact, coming straight at me!

I couldn't leave my drugged squirrels lying there unprotected, so I remained in my position with my legs crossed, working away with my gear and flying squirrels scattered about. I felt confident that whatever it was would soon catch a whiff of me, or see me, and change direction. I began to get a little more concerned when the noise became really loud and it became clear that this was a big animal without any concerns. My trail went through very thick cane or foxtail grass, so I couldn't see what the animal was until it was within about ten feet of me. It was a huge feral hog with its head down, rooting through the leaves on the forest floor as it moved. I knew the hog couldn't see or smell me, and it was about to bump right into me. Of course, that was the last thing I wanted to happen because it would have scared the daylights out of the hog, making the situation very dangerous. The first thought in my head was "I have to let it know I'm here without threatening it," so in a loud, high-pitch voice I said, "Here piggy piggy."

The hog stopped dead and it seemed that time did too. What should I do!? Crazy thoughts ran through my head. "If I climb my ladder, it will eat my squirrels (looking back, I don't know how likely that was), so I should just use the ladder to beat it over the head—no, that's a bad idea." So I basically sat there motionless, thinking that I was about to experience the worst, but not really knowing what the worst was. I was literally holding my breath, trying not to move a muscle. The hog was clearly agitated; its breathing was getting deeper so that the steam from its breath was almost reaching my face. Nothing was between us but about four feet of cane. Because of the thick cane, I couldn't see its tusks, but I wanted to know what I was up against, so I slowly tilted my head to the side in an attempt to get a clear view of its weaponry. It was apparent to me that was the instant that the hog became fully aware of my presence because as soon as I moved, it let out a hair-curling scream and turned tail and ran!

After a deep breath of relief, I finished collecting the data and put the squirrels back in the box and the box back up on the tree. While I packed up my gear, I thought about the morning's excitement and half convinced myself that the stupid hog couldn't have hurt me if it had tried. Although I already knew that I was kidding myself, as I continued to the next box, I saw the evidence of just how powerful an animal I had just met face to face. In its fright, the hog had run through a thicket of pine saplings that were about an inch in diameter. I could clearly see the path of its panicked escape from the snapped-off trees that it had left behind. Needless to say, I felt very lucky that I had avoided disaster that day, and I was convinced that I had just had the closest unintentional encounter with the biggest animal that I would ever have in my career. I turned out to be wrong on both the closest and biggest parts of that assumption.

Soon after finishing my PhD, I took a faculty job at Arkansas State University, where I planned to establish a new study with a different animal. I wanted to use nest boxes again, since they are so valuable for gaining access to lots of animals. I decided to study eastern bluebirds and proceeded to put up about two hundred boxes on private land, with landowners' cooperation, just north of Jonesboro, Arkansas. As a new assistant professor, I also needed graduate students to work on the project. Luckily, a student, T. J. Robinson, agreed to work on bluebirds for his master's research, and T. J. had over two years' experience working with eastern bluebirds.

This project was similar to the flying squirrel project in that when the birds are nesting, there can be up to six chicks in box, and from each there was a lot data to collect. We collected a blood sample and a feather sample from each, so one could spend a good deal of time at any given box. The work was very time consuming and one person could not keep up with the study population. Since field work is my first love, T. J. only had to ask for my involvement; however, we needed to standardize all of our techniques so there wouldn't be differences in our data depending upon who was taking the measurements. One of my other students, Steve Brandebura, and I met T. J. at a pasture that we knew was a productive spot for bluebirds. This particular pasture was used for raising cows, and, of course, it had one resident bull.

We already "knew" this bull, and we had been assured by the landowner that he was a lover, not a fighter. Although our observations appeared to confirm that this bull was not aggressive, we always kept an eye out for him and kept our distance when visiting his pasture. When Steve and I arrived, we met T. J. and began data collection on a box of fifteen-day-old bluebird chicks. We took our time, so T. J. could show me in great detail exactly how he was taking all the measurements. As we all sat there with our legs crossed, the bull started moving in our direction, and he seemed very curious about our presence. T. J. was sitting to my left and Steve was across from me. When the bull got within ten feet, approaching from behind me, I asked the question that we were all thinking: "Is anybody else getting a little freaked out that he's moving so close to us?"

They both agreed that this was a concern, so I asked Steve to slowly stand up to see if that deterred the animal's advance. Still he kept coming right toward us with his head down as if he wanted to see what we were doing. He got right up next to us; he was so close that T. J. reached out and petted him on his muzzle in an attempt to reassure the big guy. It was then that this huge animal turned his attention to me. Throughout all of this, I was still attempting to take measurements from a chick that I was holding; I was still sitting with my legs crossed and in no position to make a fast get away.

Finally the bull cupped his left nostril over my right shoulder and started taking deep breaths. This all happened too fast for me to really become scared, but it was very strange. I looked at my students, who were both laughing nervously while staring at me and the bull. The bull took about six or seven deep whiffs with his nostril completely encompassing my shoulder. He drew my loose-fitting shirt into his nostril with each breath, and I could feel my T-shirt tighten around my neck with each inhalation that he took. Then he stopped smelling me and just wandered off, leaving me in disbelief and my students entirely amused. One thing is for sure; I was glad he was neither a fighter nor a lover on that particular day!

Additional Readings

Brady, M. J., T. S. Risch, and F. S. Dobson. 2000. Availability of nest sites does not limit population size of southern flying squirrels. *Canadian Journal of Zoology* 78:1144–1149.

Fokidis, H. B., and T. S. Risch. 2005. The use of nest boxes to sample arboreal vertebrates. *Southeastern Naturalist* 4:447–458.

Risch, T. S., and T. J. Robinson. 2006. First observation of cavity nesting by a female blue grosbeak. *Wilson Journal of Ornithology* 118:107–108.

Robinson, T. J., L. M. Siefferman, and T. S. Risch. 2005. A quick, inexpensive trap for use with nest boxes. *North American Bird Bander* 29:115–116.

Orca Threaten, Toss Them the Dog

RICHARD GRIPPO

🙖 "WHEN I TELL YOU TO, throw that damn dog overboard!"

This was the command barked out to me by a damp, angry, native Alaskan—damp because it is almost always damp in coastal Alaska and angry because she had made a decision that she knew would be unpopular with her family. Neena Totemof was a fisherwoman and knew the difference between wanting to save the family pet and needing to save her own skin. The object of her ire was a large, wet, black Labrador retriever, barking frantically and straining against my white-knuckled hold on his collar. He wanted to leap into the frigid sea and have at the large marine mammals steadily gaining on our little skiff with its meager 10-horsepower "kicker." *He* was not going to let them have us for lunch . . .

"How the heck did I get myself into this predicament?" I wondered. How the heck, indeed.

This story begins in 1989, when the new supertanker *Exxon Valdez,* loaded with over 1.2 million barrels of Prudhoe Bay crude oil, grounded in the Gulf of Alaska's Prince William Sound. The Sound is an area of extreme isolation, pristine beauty, and incredible ecological diversity. For eleven years, oil tankers had been successfully negotiating the rocky passage out of the port of Valdez and through the Valdez Narrows, a 1,700-yard-wide channel that forms the entrance to Valdez Bay. But on March 23, luck ran out on *Exxon,* in the form of icebergs calving off of Columbia Glacier and drifting into the Valdez tanker lanes. It was a little after midnight; the supertanker had just been topped off with Alaskan pipeline oil and was headed to a refinery in California. Trying to avoid the slowly drifting icebergs, Captain Hazelwood turned the 1,000-foot steel leviathan into the inbound shipping lane. For reasons still unclear, the *Exxon Valdez* did not turn back, steamed completely through the inbound lane, and with a metallic moan grounded on Bligh Island reef. For three days the ship lay on Bligh reef, unable to move and equally unable to stem the bubbling cauldron of oil escaping into the sea at the rate of 20,000 gallons per hour and forming an ever-enlarging oil slick around the stricken vessel. Eventually, 11 million gallons of oil escaped from the *Exxon Valdez*. For three days the wind remained calm in Prince William Sound, the oil just sitting there in the gentle swell, waiting for human acknowledgment, for action, for redemption.

Spills happen. But cleanups are supposed to happen too, in the form of oil skimmers, containment booms, surfactants to disperse the oil, and even fire if the spill is fresh enough to ignite the highly flammable volatiles comprising 30 percent of fresh crude oil. In this case, an effective cleanup effort by Alyeska, the consortium of six oil companies that owned the Trans-Alaskan Pipeline, did not materialize until too late. After three days of grace, during which chaos reigned over the spill response, a spring blizzard boiled out of the Chugach Mountains and strong winds began whipping the oil across Prince William Sound, out Hutchinbrook Passage, and into the Gulf of Alaska. The Alaska current, driven primarily by the physical interaction between the freshwater disgorged by the numerous coastal rivers and the salty ocean water, moved the oil down the Kenai Peninsula toward Cook Inlet, Kodiak Island, and beyond. Over one thousand miles of coastline were eventually baptized by oil in a greasy line extending from Prince William Sound to the northern Aleutian Islands and up into lower Cook Inlet. The ecological toll was unprecedented, made all the more intolerable by the pristine conditions usually prevailing in this region of the world.

Alaskans got mad. Real mad. Maybe too mad, considering they had no state income tax due to the taxes on the profits resulting from the Alaskan pipeline (between 1969 and 1987 a healthy $464,144 per hour *after* taxes for the parent companies). So, instead of sending a check to the state capital at tax time, every Alaskan man, woman, and child received a check amounting to at least $800 every year. However, as any ecologist knows, there ain't no such thing as a free lunch. The payment comes in the form of environmental degradation due to oil exploration, road and drill rig construction, and spills. However, no one in his worst nightmare could foresee the extent of the disaster caused by a single ship. So, Alaskans owning shorelines directly impacted by the spill wanted to sue Exxon and

Alyeska. Local attorneys quickly realized that to have any kind of chance against Exxon in court they would need to initiate a class action and file suit on behalf of their many groups or classes of clients, such as Alaskan natives, commercial fishermen, or shoreline property owners. Up until that point in time, the biggest environmental class action had been the suit associated with the Three Mile Island nuclear accident in Pennsylvania. So, the Alaskan attorneys contacted the Philadelphia attorneys that handled that case and the Exxon Valdez Oil Spill class action was spawned. The lead law firm organizing the class action started looking around the country for scientific support of their case, mainly in the form of expert witnesses. All of the usual marine ecotoxicological experts were already retained/aligned with either Exxon, the federal government, or the State of Alaska. So the firm started calling universities, looking for someone to send to Alaska and gather evidence to be used against Exxon . . .

Ah, finally back to me. At the time of the spill, I was an involved graduate student, working on my PhD in ecology at Pennsylvania State University. I was primarily working on the development of an ecotoxicological bio-indicator of coal mine pollution using the physiological responses of aquatic organisms. I had earned a BS in marine biology in 1978 and an MS in marine ecology in '80, but up until the winter of 1990, I had really not had much contact with the ocean, except for vacations. That winter, however, my doctoral advisor and I had organized and taught a course, Tropical Field Ecology, in Belize, Central America. The class spent a week in the rainforest of the Cockscomb Jaguar Preserve in the Mayan Mountains bordering Belize and Guatemala, then a week on one of the barrier islands off the Belizean coast, part of the world's second longest barrier reef. I was in charge of the marine portion of the course, so I was freshly boned up on marine ecosystems and how humans are affecting them.

When the phone call came from the lawyer, he was actually looking for my advisor, Bill Dunson, a world-renowned physiological ecologist who had worked as chief scientist on several *Alpha Helix* marine research cruises, to serve as an expert witness. The lawyer explained to me that they were looking for someone to send to Alaska, to look at the shorelines of their clients and determine the extent of ecological damage, if any, that could be attributed to oiling by the *Exxon Valdez*. The modus operandi would be for the expert to be dropped off with camping gear at various sites by fishing boat, bush plane, or helicopter, establish research sites, and collect data. After a week or so, the expert would be picked up and flown to the next site. He mentioned something about bears and guns and rain and sea otters, but all I could think of was how lucky my advisor was to be offered such an opportunity. However, Wild Bill, as he was affectionately called by his students, was unavailable. He was in Virginia on Chincoteague Island. He had a house there that doubled as a marine lab, and during the summers, he spent as much time as he could on the island. After promising the lawyer I would talk to my advisor and also ask around Penn State to see if anyone else might want to do it, I hung up. I tracked down the Chincoteague phone number and called Bill.

"You are never going to guess who just called!" I told him excitedly. "A lawyer involved with the *Exxon Valdez* lawsuit wants you to go to Alaska and collect evidence. He wants you to camp on the beach and swim in the ocean and collect dead sea otters," I said. There was a moment of silence at the other end of the line.

"The ocean water in Alaska is just above freezing, even in summer," he spoke dryly. "If you go into that water you will die a quick and painful death. Freeze to death in about five minutes." Unbeknownst to me, at that precise moment in time Bill was lying in a hammock on his back porch, enjoying the warm bay sunset and balmy breezes of coastal Virginia. "I don't want to go to Alaska and collect rotting carcasses. It's cold up there," he stated matter-of-factly. "Actually, the otters would all be gone, dragged off by scavengers. To determine any impact of the oil, one would have to look at something more permanent, something to do with the rocky intertidal," he mused. Suddenly he stopped and said, "But *you* could do it! Don't you have a couple of degrees in marine biology? Plus you are now training to be an ecotoxicologist. They would go together perfectly for this job. It will be great experience for you if they pay you enough to make up for the time you will be missing from your own research."

Be paid to go to Alaska, camp on the beaches, and look at wildlife?! The thought of anyone being paid to do this had never crossed by mind. I had truly believed Bill would be doing it for the fun of it, the adventure. A free trip to Alaska! Wasn't that enough payment? Why would anyone expect to get more out of this than that? However, the thought of "easy" money made me quickly come to my senses.

"How much do you think they would pay?" I asked. I really had no idea what an expert witness made: $10 or $12 an hour? As an exercise in depression, we graduate students had once worked out, based on our meager salaries, how much we were being paid to work sixty- to seventy-hour weeks. It came to $2.71 per hour with no overtime.

"Why don't you charge them what you got paid for teaching the Belize class? We taught the class over three weeks so that would be $1,000 a week," he said, sounding pleased that he had thought up such a great deal.

And $1,000 a week! To go to Alaska! My head was reeling. It was true that I had been paid $3,000 for the three-week duration of the class, but that undertaking included many weeks of preparation on everything from booking flights for twenty-five people to working up a clothing checklist. This was different. I just knew there would not be much preparation to go to Alaska . . .

"My advisor can't go. But I found someone else who can," I said to the lawyer the next day. "Me! I have training in marine biology and eco-toxicology. I am actually the perfect person for the job!"

"What would your fee be?" he asked. I had been afraid that he would quiz me extensively on what I knew about the environmental impact of oil spills (I knew virtually nothing). Instead, he had gotten right to the heart of the matter. It was my first lesson in how trial lawyers think.

"I will charge $1,000 per week," I said and held my breath. Would he go for such an outlandish fee? Little did I know that a good Philadelphia lawyer generates that much in fees by lunchtime of a typical work day.

"What about your expenses? How much for food?" he asked. This took me off guard. I thought the fee covered my food. Thinking quickly, I doubled the typical per diem given to graduate students: $50 per day. I knew Alaska was expensive, but I had no idea if that number was reasonable. I figured if it was low, I would just eat peanut butter on the beaches.

"That's starting to get a little high!" he said. Little did I know that by tradition lawyers groused about how much experts charged for meals. I guess they must figure it is better to keep them hungry, make them work harder.

"It's expensive in Alaska," I said firmly. Where was this conviction coming from? Certainly not from experience. I had never been there!

"OK, OK, $50 dollars a day, except for when you are flying to and from Alaska. Then it is only $25 because they give you meals on the plane." This, of course, was back in the time when flying was elegant, back before you had to pay for your little bags of pretzels. "And I will pay you $25 an hour to prepare for the trip and to prepare the report when you get back," he said.

"One other thing. You are going to need to bring a gun for the bears. In case they try to eat you. A shotgun with triple 0 buckshot would be best," he added calmly. It was as if every day he told his employees to bring a lethal weapon to work.

"What if I brought a 45-caliber pistol instead," I asked, thinking it would be a lot lighter and easier to handle.

"If you bring that you will have to saw off the front sight," he said with a chuckle. "That way, when that big ol' bear takes that pistol away from you and shoves it up your ass, it won't hurt so much! You have to bring something with stopping power. A charging bear will generate a couple of tons of force that will have to be stopped dead in its tracks, or you will be dead. A pistol will just get it mad."

"Oh," I said.

When I tell people I went to Alaska as an environmental consultant, the response is invariably, "I always wanted to go to Alaska but I never have."

I always respond, "You should go. It's easy to go to Alaska."

I am lying, of course. It is not easy to go to Alaska, at least not if you are going to collect data on the "beaches," in the rain, at midnight, with the possibility of a grizzly bear peering over your shoulder, wondering if what you are doing will produce something good for them to eat. Maybe wondering if *you* are good to eat. The possibility of hungry bears wandering upon the scene changes everything. You have to carry a loaded shotgun strapped to your shoulder while you clamber up and down boulders and rocks that make up the typical Alaskan shoreline.

Most hunters will think I am a wimp to whine about having to carry a shotgun. Most hunters have also never walked for sixteen hours in a rain suit and hip boots in the drizzle with guns strapped to their backs, wondering if that noise they heard was a spruce ptarmigan looking for a lady ptarmigan or a grizzly licking its chops.

In addition to a gun, I had to collect and organize a large pile of sampling gear, including glass collection bottles, hip boots and rain suit, notebooks, chisels for scraping barnacles and mussels off rocks, cameras, extra shotgun shells to fight off the bear armies, and, of course, all my clothing, camping gear, and food. I had to make dozens of phone calls to lawyers, scientists from universities, consulting firms, state and federal agencies, and Native Alaskan corporations (municipalities). I booked airline flights, bush plane flights, helicopter charters, ferries, water taxis, hotel rooms, and remote wilderness campsites in national forests. When I finally got my itinerary, equipment, and supplies together, I flew first to Anchorage to meet the local attorneys, get my bearings, and chat with the Alaska Departments of Natural Resources (DNR), Fish and Game, and Environmental Conservation, the U.S. Fish and Wildlife Service, and other local organizations and oil spill offices about the latest happenings regarding the spill. Most people were helpful, although a bit concerned that I was going out to the shorelines by myself. The personnel at the DNR were generally ecstatic that someone would be evaluating a portion of the hundreds of impacted shorelines in Prince William Sound for oil damage because they, like most states' agencies, were seriously undermanned for such a monumental task.

Anchorage was an interesting town. Alaska has about five hundred thousand residents and about half of them live in Anchorage. Nestled between the coastal Chugach Mountain range and foggy Cook Inlet, it is a town of startling contrasts. Grizzled fishermen walk down the streets in front of shop windows displaying $14,000 works of Alaskan art. The same fishermen might be found sitting in seafood restaurants, paying $29.95 for a pound of king crab after they had just finished working almost non-stop for two weeks in the Bering Sea catching 150,000 pounds of the leggy critters.

You can see the latest, hopped-up, Asian sports coupes purring down the streets and crossing over the painted line that is used for the snowy start of the Iditarod dogsled race that ends 1,050 miles away in Nome, where they celebrate the winner with a reindeer potluck dinner and ice golf. In a typical example of Alaskan irony, a Mexican restaurant has opened its doors right across from the starting line of arguably the world's coldest sporting event.

Even though I visited in the summer, hints of the severe winters were everywhere, such as the electrical plugs that dangled out the front grill of most cars. These are used to plug in the two or three heaters in the engine block, oil pan, and radiator to keep the vehicle from freezing to death. Many stores have electrical outlets in their parking lots to which customers can plug their cars while they are stocking up on supplies. You would think that with all the bad weather, long cold winters, and lack of sunlight from November to March that the locals would be a dour, depressed, taciturn lot. Instead, Alaskans are among the friendliest people I have ever met (with the exception of some of the bush pilots). They are proud of their state and seem to be avidly promoting tourism and want to make each visitor's stay in the Last Frontier as rewarding as possible. Perhaps they realize that the cash cow that is oil revenue will not last forever . . .

When I finally left Anchorage and arrived by air taxi at the city of Cordova on Prince William Sound, the bush pilot took one look at my pile of stuff and said, "Usually we charge for the passenger and their gear comes free. In your case, I think we should charge for the gear and throw you in for free."

Before the bush plane would take off there were always several minor emergencies happening simultaneously. Usually, the pilot was yelling about how my stuff weighed too much, and we would probably die trying to take off and definitely die trying to land. To make flying worse, the pilots were always muttering about how a bad weather front was coming into exactly where we needed to go. This was mildly amusing because often the pilot did not know exactly where we needed to go. Fortunately, the resolution of this particular dilemma was close at hand. A sleek Mercedes or some other type of lawyer-car would be idling nearby. Several lawyers would be staring intently at the back seat, where a satellite-radio-type thing would be sitting and whirring and belching forth lawyer-sized pieces of paper covered with indecipherable hieroglyphics. These turned out to be sections of a map of the particular landowner whose shoreline I was going to inspect. The lawyers would thrust the papers at me through the window of the plane as the pilot, finally having lost all patience with me, my stuff, the lawyers, and the looming weather, started taxiing down the runway or pulling away from the dock. I was left sitting in the passenger seat, searching for a seat belt while trying to piece together the paper puzzle into some sort of readable whole. This was very important because we had to find the correct island, cove, or shoreline. It would do no one any good if the pilot set me down on the wrong property for three or four days. With no radio with which to call the pilot back, all I would have been able to do was sit and watch my food supply get smaller.

Flying in bush planes was fun, sort of. Actually, much of the time it was terrifying. Bush pilots are a different breed. They basically use airplanes like pickup trucks, and we all know how well most pickups are driven. Bush pilots fly about the same way. Actually, flying is not so bad. But the landings make you wonder what happened to them in their youth to cause them to see the world so differently. They never ever say no to landing in the most unimaginable places, like on a gravely beach between two trees, and going through a pod of Stellar sea lions, which scatter like bowling pins and never seem to get bonked by the plane. This is good, considering that Stellar sea lions are considered an endangered species in Alaska. Most of the time bush planes land in water. Water slows the plane down very fast, so it was not unusual for the pilot to scream ten feet over the treetops at 100 knots, bank sharply to head into the wind, and slam down into the sea like a reentering Apollo space capsule. Water would spray up on both sides of the plane and it would stop in about the length of a football field. Many times we would land in the narrow part of some protected bay, and after dropping me off, the pilot would have to taxi for five minutes to get out of the bay and into the open sea to have enough room to take off.

If the waves were running high, as the aircraft neared the water, the pilot would violently yank up the nose of the plane to avoid landing on the down slope of a wave, which could cause the plane to nose down into the wave trough and flip over. The next second, the plane would just as violently be yanked up to hit the next oncoming wave upslope, pontoons first. It took two occurrences of me crunching my face on the dashboard (now I know why they call it that) before I learned to put my feet up on the dashboard, lean way back, and forcefully hold my head against the seat. So there I would be, feet up and braced against the dash, hands clutching at the handholds, head back, probably with a look of terror in my eyes—which were closed.

My stomach, of course, was still in the treetops.

The pilot would then gingerly taxi up to the rocky shoreline. There are no beaches in Alaska where I went, only rocks, boulders, and gravel. The waves could lift up the plane and smash it down onto the rocks at any moment, so the pilot was always in a hurry to get away from shore and would just stand on a pontoon and start tossing my stuff onto the rocks without looking up. If I was not there to catch the stuff, it would just splat down on the rocks, the shallows, wherever gravity took it. My camping gear could handle the insult, but the cases of glass sample bottles were fragile. I learned to carry two cases because invariably one would end up full of broken bottles. As the plane taxied away, my pile of stuff, which had appeared huge in the airplane, looked very small on shore.

Once on the shoreline, my first item of business was always the same—load the shotgun and man the battle stations! Bears generally run away from the sound of bush planes, but I was told that some come back to see if the humans had anything good to eat. Or maybe to see if the *humans* were good to eat. After the beachhead was secure, it was time to set up camp, which basically meant extracting the two-man backpacking tent from the increasingly wet pile of equipment. It is not fun setting up a tent by oneself in windy rain, especially when the one is operating at top speed because the longer it took to set up, the more bath-like the inside of the tent became. Finally, after struggling with tent poles and stakes and the fly (called this, I think, because it liked to fly away in the wind and plaster itself up against a tree just out of my reach), I would get into the tent, unpack the sleeping bag, and get in it to warm up. And think about how I was going to find some dry wood to start a fire because putting a wet body into a damp sleeping bag is not a very good way to warm up. Eventually, my violent shivering made it obvious that I was either going to have to find wood and build a fire or die of hypothermia. It is not easy finding dry wood in a steady drizzle, but it is easier than dying, so out I would go. I looked for downed trees; I looked under them for branches held up off the ground and also sheltered by the tree itself. These semi-dry branches could be coaxed into flame with a little help from stove fuel. Boy Scouts would frown on my fire-starting methods, but I would be looking at flames hours before they could get a fire started by rubbing two sticks together. After warming myself at the sputtering, smoky fire, it was time to get into the rain suit, pull on the hip boots, grab the map pieces and a compass, and head out to the shoreline.

The first thing any scientific expert amassing evidence for a lawsuit must do is establish the location from which the evidence is collected. In my case I needed to evaluate particular shoreline properties for damage ostensibly arising from oil deposited by the *Exxon Valdez* spill. Thus, showing that I was, in fact, on the correct landowner's property was critical. The "other side" will always challenge the admissibility of any evidence by compelling the scientist to prove that he/she was on the correct property. In my case it was not always easy to show I was even on the correct island because I had to try to determine where I was going by looking at faxed map sections held at arm's length in the cramped compartment of a bush plane while the pilot was cursing and playing air tag with seagulls and murres. The best evidence is often a picture; it is usually unequivocal and not subject to different interpretations by dueling scientific experts. Most properties had boundary markers; I just had to locate the two markers on the shoreline at each end of the property. Generally, this meant slopping through the wet underbrush, tide pools, mudflats, whatever, and peering under bushes, on trees, etc., until I found the marker and then taking pictures of it from several angles, preferably with me and the ocean in the background (to prove that I was actually there). Some properties did not have boundary markers but rather a legal document called a "metes and bounds" description. These were composed of crude maps and text describing the property boundaries, such as "property extends westerly from the west corner of cabin for a distance of 433 feet along the mean high-tide line and easterly for 167 feet from the east corner of the cabin." I would take pictures of the cabin and a tape measure deployed along the high-tide mark, indicating that the boundaries of the property were measured correctly.

Finally, some parts of Alaska have no legal description because they are not under the jurisdiction of the United States but rather are part of the Native Alaskan lands that were never deeded over to the U.S. government at the time of Seward's Folly. The only legally defendable characteristic of these properties was the topography. Pictures taken from the air showing streams, coastline, hills, river mouths, etc. would be matched up to topographic maps to prove that I was at the correct location. It was a bit of an ego rush to tell two Vietnam-veteran helicopter pilots, chartered at $800 per hour to provide transportation to sites so remote and rugged that bush planes and boats could not be used, to "turn the chopper a little to the left and tilt down slightly" to get a good picture of the shoreline property. The pilots "got me back" later that day when we had to stop on Augustine Island in southern Cook Inlet to refuel the helicopter from a fuel cache on the island. The pilots seemed to be a bit nervous and tentative on the approach, possibly because they were concerned about being blown onto the tall, cone-shaped mountain that dominates the island. We finally touched down, and I sat in the helicopter while the two pilots wrestled drums of fuel close to the aircraft and started the pump rig to transfer fuel from the drums into the helicopter. Looking around, I noticed that we were more or less surrounded by these drums of helicopter fuel. Looking up, I also noticed that a cloud formation at the summit that I had seen on the way in had not moved, in spite of the rather stiff winds that were usually prevalent in Cook Inlet. As the pilots finished up refueling and we readied for takeoff, I asked what fuel was used for helicopters, expecting them to say some special type of high-octane gasoline or diesel.

"Helicopters run on jet fuel," one of them replied. "Our company has about seventy-five barrels on the island. Other helicopter charter services also store fuel here, so there are about three hundred barrels of jet fuel altogether."

The other pilot added, "I think the military base out of Anchorage also stores fuel here. They probably have a lot, like six hundred to seven hundred barrels. There could be as many as a thousand barrels of jet fuel on this rock."

"Cool," I thought, "as long as no one lights a match."

"I also noticed that the clouds around here do not seem to be moving much," I said brightly. "Is there some kind of strange weather pattern around the island?"

"What are you talking about?" the first pilot asked.

"Look up at the top of the mountain; the clouds are not moving," I said helpfully.

"Oh, that," he said. "They are not moving because they are not clouds. That is steam coming from the volcano. Augustine is a volcano."

I gulped. Volcano! I looked around at the drums of jet fuel.

"When was the last time it was active?" I asked, half fearful of the answer.

"Oh, it hasn't blown for three or four years. 'Bout time for it to go again, I guess," he answered casually as he hit the starter button for the rotors.

After delineating the property, it was time to do science. Because most marine scientists capable of providing support for this litigation had aligned with either the plaintiffs or defendants (Exxon, Alyeska) the consortium of lawyers handling the private class-action suit had to scramble for "experts" from what was left. So, I was actually recruited as a scientific leftover, kind of like a turkey sandwich the day after Thanksgiving. Sending me up there was really a tremendous risk for the attorneys; not only was I an unproven quantity (just a *student,* after all), but I was operating alone. Normally, a team of scientists and field technicians would descend on a shoreline like over-paid ants, set up a sampling grid within the intertidal zone, and start surveying within defined sampling areas called quadrants. If many shorelines needed to be evaluated, the team would fly in, take pictures of the quadrants and evaluate them later to identify the organisms present. If the pictures turned out badly or needed to be ground-truthed, the team could come back later and evaluate the shoreline at their leisure. I needed to evaluate the shorelines on the spot; there was probably no coming back, and I could not risk taking pictures and realizing that they were not good when I was back at school four thousand miles away. So I had to devise a way to get the job done without help, in a minimum amount of time, and with only the equipment that would fit into a bush plane.

When I first starting inspecting the shorelines, I noticed that on the unoiled shorelines the size (diameter) of the acorn barnacle, *Balanus glandula,* was related to the intertidal zone (vertical distance from low tide to high tide) in which they occurred. This seemed to be due to the time spent underwater during each cycle of the tide; the longer they were in the water, the longer they could feed during any given tidal cycle. Thus, the barnacles in the lower intertidal areas were larger, those in the middle intertidal were of an intermediate size, and those located on the upper intertidal were smallest. On those rocky shorelines that showed signs of oiling, all of the *B. glandula* were of approximately the same small size, as if the rocks had been cleared all at once in all intertidal zones, and then larval barnacles had recolonized the rocks in all tidal zones at approximately the same time. Thus, lack of size stratification along intertidal zones seemed to be an indicator of ecological impact due to oiling; the existence of stratification by size indicated no oiling. This was a nice technique to use; barnacles are easy to measure, mostly because they just sit there and do not try to run away.

Because this idea had not yet been scientifically scrutinized by peer-reviewed publication, I also performed a standard intertidal-survey analysis on a subset of the quadrants to correlate changes in barnacle size (or lack thereof) with changes in diversity and species richness that followed patterns expected from oil-spill impact. I needed all the corroborating evidence I could muster to counter the assertion by the defense's scientific experts that my sampling design, collection methods, oil-sample analyses, etc. were incorrect, and thus all my data were flawed. I was told that no matter what I did, the other side would be able to find someone to refute what I found and said. The basic reality for scientific support is that for every PhD, there is an equal and opposite PhD. It would be up to me to convince the judge or jury that my interpretation made for the most convincing argument.

When I found the distribution of barnacles by size to be affected, it was time to break out the (unbroken) sample bottles and collect some oil to connect any ecological differences found with the presence of actual *Exxon Valdez* oil. By determining the ratios among the thousands of hydrocarbons contained in a crude oil sample, a close match to the oil spilled by the *Exxon Valdez* could be obtained, a process known as forensic spill-source matching. Each case of glass sample bottles was certified by the manufacturer to be absolutely free of any chemicals whatsoever. However, I needed to show that just opening a sample bottle on a site did not cause contamination by crude oil from a bush plane, helicopter, or errant seagull dropping. So every so often a sample would consist of simply opening a sample bottle, exposing it to the air for about the same length of time as it usually took to collect an oil sample, and sealing it back up. This would subsequently be analyzed just like any sample bottle. When I first explained this to the lawyer, he went ballistic.

"You mean I have to pay $300 to analyze a sample bottle that we know is empty?"

"Yeah," I said, "Every tenth bottle has to be a field control. Just open it, expose it to air, seal it, and analyze it just like the rest of 'em. Have to prove that there was no *Exxon Valdez* oil in the air or coming from the copter exhaust or somehow slipped in there by someone."

"Hmm" he said, unbelieving. "I'll get back to you on that one."

Apparently he checked with someone who knew what forensic spill-source matching was all about because he gave the OK for me to collect an extra $3,000 worth of samples. Or as he put it, "$3,000 of worthless samples."

Finally, after the oil samples had been collected, the bottles were sealed with evidence tape. This was a special kind of sticky tape that could not be removed without tearing it to bits. By putting my signature on the evidence tape and signing a manifest sheet, I would start a chain-of-custody that would extend from a shoreline in Alaska, back by bush plane to Anchorage, to the "Lower 48," and finally to the oil-analysis laboratory at Texas A&M University, where analytical scientists would determine if the samples collected were consistent with an *Exxon Valdez* origin (many were).

Working on Alaskan shorelines can be tricky. As a matter of survival, one becomes intimately familiar with the tide tables. Because the tides change so much in the Arctic (up to twenty-five feet every six hours), one must follow the tide tables and get out on the shorelines when the tide is down. That sometimes put me on the sampling site at 1:00 AM until 3:00 AM, then again at 7:00 AM to 10:00 AM, all the way up to around midnight. The fact that in that part of Alaska in the summer the sun sets at about 11:30 PM and rises again at 3:00 AM made these middle of the night forays much easier to take. It also made for changes in my work and meal habits. Many were the times that I stopped to look at my watch because the hunger pangs were starting to get severe, and I was astonished to realize that it was after 10:00 PM at night! I was amazed not so much that I was working that late (a typical work time for a graduate student) but that I had actually worked through dinner (not typical for me).

As the tide comes up you also have to make sure you will not be cut off and stranded by the rising water with no place to go except up a thirty-foot cliff. This only happened to me once. I was surveying my way around a section of shoreline called Knowles Point in the Knight Island Passage that connects Prince William Sound with Montague Straight and eventually the rest of the Gulf of Alaska. According to the map, I was on a small peninsula and should have ended up back close to where I started my survey at a narrow section of the point. Instead, the shoreline simply narrowed down to the sea at the base of a tall cliff that bordered the coast for at least a mile. After looking at the map for a while, trying to figure out where it had all gone wrong, I turned around to start back, but I immediately realized that the tide had risen behind my back and was continuing to rise too fast for me to make it back to the point where the cliffs ended and I could scramble inland. What to do? After staring at the sea for a few moments, I dropped all my gear and my gun (screw the evidence, I wanted to live) and started back on a dead run in my hip boots, hoping I could somehow outpace the tide. As I started to breath heavily, I rounded a corner and there, unnoticed when approaching from my original direction of survey, was a wonderful, beautiful trail leading up the bluff and into the forest above. Turning, I ran back to get my gear and gun (save the evidence, I wanted to get paid) and sprinted back to the trail. Huffing and puffing, I started up the trail. It was a bit slippery, and I noticed a foul odor, kind of like a cat box after feeding the kitty nothing but cans of Saucy Salmon Surprise for two weeks because cat food is cheaper by the case. As I entered the trees, I noticed that some of them appeared scratched as if by a large cat. With a start, I realized that the trail I was on was not a hiking trail. It was a bear trail. The scratches were from grizzly bears, sharpening their claws in case a graduate student should wander upon the scene. I immediately un-shouldered my shotgun, slipped the safety off, and held it up at the ready. I tried to remember what the various helpful Alaskans had told me about avoiding bears. Rule number one: do not surprise them. I started singing loudly and badly. Loudly, so the bears would know I was coming. Badly, so they would run away when they heard me (just like the audiences for my oldies band). Apparently, it worked, because no bears came to see if I had or was anything good to eat.

Working on the shorelines was actually fun once I got used to being continually damp. Where else could one do a job while viewing bald eagles, Dall sheep and mountain goats, puffins, sea lions, and the occasional killer whale? But after several weeks, I found myself on Peak Island, one of dozens of small rocky islands that had stood directly in the path of the spreading oil slick during the first days of the spill. The island was approximately crescent shaped, rising up out of Prince William Sound like a croissant covered with trees.

I had been working pretty much continuously, often putting in eighteen-hour days. It was time to take a break. What does one do after spending weeks splashing through the waves and tide and rain with water as your near-constant companion? Why, go fishing, of course. And how does one go fishing after getting around in fishing boats and bush planes and helicopters? Why, take a small skiff into the big ocean. At least that's what I did.

The only other persons on Peak Island were a fisherman with his wife and small daughter in a small cabin they used during the summer fishing

Peak Island Inlet.
PHOTOGRAPH BY RICHARD GRIPPO.

season. The rest of the island was a part of the Chugach National Forest. The wife, Neena Totemof, was the great granddaughter of Alice Clock, the original homesteader of Peak Island in the 1920s. At that time the island was used as a place to raise arctic foxes for the commercial fur industry. The foxes roamed free over the entire island but were fed with fish placed into wire cages with the doors held open. The homesteaders had even hollowed a series of small caves in the base of the main hill to increase the number of burrows available to the foxes. When it was time to harvest the foxes, the doors were rigged to close after the foxes entered to feed. The remains of the cave dens and feeding\capture cages can still be found on the island.

I like to fish. As I worked the shorelines, I could hear and even occasionally see salmon jumping and splashing the water's surface four hundred to five hundred feet off shore as they migrated along the coast. I could not reach them by casting from shore, but maybe Neena would let me borrow the skiff? I explained to her that while earning my master's degree I had worked as a teaching assistant at a marine lab in the U.S. Virgin Islands, where my primary duty had been to take students on field trips around St. Croix in a scuba boat and go diving with them. I had a lot of experience with small boats and thought I could handle just about anything the ocean could throw at me. As it turned out, I really had no idea what the Alaskan sea could produce.

After a long pause she said, "The tide gets pretty tricky between Peak and Naked [islands], and that's where you have to go to get to the best place for salmon. Why don't I drive the skiff and you can just fish?"

I was slightly taken aback, but it was her boat. I sensed that there was something else besides tidal currents on her mind but did not want to pry and jeopardize my chance to fish for the fabled Alaskan salmon—for free! People pay thousands of dollars to fly to Alaska and fish for salmon and halibut. All I had to do was agree that Neena would accompany me and captain the boat. It was a no-brainer. I ran and got my fishing gear while Neena readied the boat. Just as we finished loading up and were getting ready to cast off from the tiny dock in front of the cabin, a large black Labrador retriever came running down the path carrying something in his mouth. As he approached, he appeared to be carrying some type of bird.

"Oh damn, the dog has found a ptarmigan nest again," Neena said unhappily. Neena was a bird lover, not unusual when one spends a lot of time on an almost abandoned island in a birders' paradise. Apparently, these particular birds were easy to catch with easy-to-find nests that were located on the ground. These ptarmigan were even called "idiot birds" by some of the natives. Kenai (that's the name of the dog) had a bad habit of finding the nests and destroying all the eggs or chicks after catching the mother, which is what he now held in his mouth.

Neena hesitated a second, then called to the dog to jump into the skiff, which he happily did. I thought it made things a bit crowded, but Neena just muttered something about it being quiet out today and not seeing any for a while and pulled on the starter rope. After two or three pulls, the motor sputtered to life and we were off, Neena at the back working the kicker, me in the middle with my fishing pole, and Kenai the dog happily occupying the front seat, head up, ears flapping back in the wind, and tongue lolling out. We pulled out of the small bay and entered the channel between Peak and Naked Islands. Everything looked calm to me as we moved down the channel to the other side of the island.

"Cast over there, about a hundred feet off those rocks," she said. I thought it was too close to the shore but did what I was told. I immediately got a strike and hooked into something big and strong underwater. The spinning pole bent into a question mark and line stripped off the reel as the drag screamed. Neena handled the skiff expertly, turning, twisting, or backing up to keep us parallel to the fish while simultaneously working the boat in the direction of the fish to help recover the line that had zipped off the reel during several long runs. I had my hands full fighting the fish and quickly realized that this was not a one-person job. Without Neena's assistance, I would have assuredly lost the fish. It took a full ten minutes, but I finally brought the fish to the boat. It was a beautiful, silvery, chinook salmon, probably weighing twenty-five to thirty pounds. It looked huge alongside the boat and even larger after Neena grabbed the net and had me lead the salmon into it. As I leaned the other way, she lifted the fish out of the water and dropped it into the boat.

"That's a nice king," she said. "When we get back, we'll build a fire from some alder I collected, and I will show you how to smoke salmon. Then we'll dry it in my cabin. You can take some back with you. In fact, let's try to get your limit (two fish), and you can take a lot back."

We went back to the spot where I had caught the fish. As I prepared to start casting, I asked Neena why this particular spot was good for fishing so close to shore.

"There is a deep drop-off near shore right here and some big boulders about thirty feet down. We usually can pick up one or two fish from this area," she said.

However, my beginner's luck did not hold out. In spite of twenty minutes of steady casting and retrieval, all I caught was a small, black-and-red-striped, sea-robin-looking thing.

"Aah!" Neena said disgustedly. "Those things are no good. Only Russians eat them. Russians will eat anything they catch." She sounded a bit contemptuous, perhaps forgetting a significant part of her heritage.

"This area is no good right now," she decided. "Let's go to another spot I know of near Naked!"

We turned and headed straight off shore, back toward the channel. I noticed the boat was moving a lot faster now and realized the changing tide had turned the channel into an ocean interstate. The tide was helping to take us where we needed to go. I'm sure Neena had planned for this when she took me out. But, she had not planned for what happened next . . .

As I was gazing to the left over the water I felt the skiff jerk slightly, and Neena said something that sounded a lot like "Oh sit!" I turned around to look at her and saw that her gaze was fixed on something ahead and off to the right of the boat. I looked in that direction and at first could see nothing but choppy water. Then suddenly a short spout of water rose sharply into the air.

It was a killer whale! Cool! In fact, there was a whole pod of whales, five or six at least. Double cool! They were headed up the channel, against the tide, in a direction that would pass in front of our boat. I was going to get a chance to see them pretty close up. I immediately grabbed my camera and took a picture, then stood up to get one at a better angle.

"Orca! Get down!" Neena hissed between clenched teeth. It seemed like she was trying to be quiet and unobtrusive even though the kicker was making plenty of noise, and I was sure the orcas could hear it. The next comment took me by surprise.

"Don't let the dog see them!" she hissed again. As this second round of hissing sunk in, I wondered why she cared if the dog saw the whales. Why was whale watching bad for retrievers? At that precise instant, before I could react to what Neena said, I got the answer to my unspoken question. Kenai the dog caught sight of the whales and immediately began barking loudly. The pod, which had been moving more or less in a direction perpendicular and ahead of the boat, swung around and headed straight toward us. Neena reacted instantly, looking toward Naked Island, then back toward Peak. Wordlessly, she swung the skiff in a tight arc and headed directly away from the killer whales, back toward Peak Island, where we had just been fishing.

Kenai, in an attempt to get closer to the whales, abandoned his primo spot at the front of the skiff and tried to jump past me and into the back with Neena.

"Grab him!" she screamed. There was not a trace of hysteria in her voice. I lunged and just managed to bear hug the dog in mid-air. Kenai fell on top of me and I grabbed at his collar. We both came up panting and facing Neena at the back of the boat. I still wasn't sure what all the fuss was about, although I was a bit uneasy that the whales had decided to go in the same direction as us. Neena must have read the look on my face.

"They are chasing us!" she yelled loudly but calmly. "They think my dog is a seal or a sea lion. If they catch us they may breach and land on the boat, trying to knock him into the water. They weigh about ten thousand tons."

I knew she meant pounds, not tons, but it did not matter. Five tons of whale was more than enough to sink our little boat. Killer whales are not considered man-eaters, but once we were all thrashing around in the icy water, they probably would not be too fussy about the difference between a mammal with flippers and whiskers and one with hands and a moustache.

So there we were, bouncing across the cold sea, dog barking, prop churning, whales gracefully and silently swimming in an undulating motion behind us. I thought I could pick out some smaller fins. A whole whale family was chasing us, having some good old Alaskan fun. Chase the people and the dog.

"Are they gaining on us?" Neena asked. I realized I could see them but she could not. Up until that point I had not considered the possibility that we would not be able to easily outrun the orcas. After all, we were being propelled by a motor! What sea creature was faster than a speeding skiff? I did not know it at the time, but killer whales are extremely fast, much faster than your average Flipper-type porpoise, capable of hitting speeds of 30 mph for short bursts. I peered at the pod. Could it be? Was it possible? Yes, they were definitely gaining on us! I could not believe it. Neena could see in my eyes what the answer to her question was. I could then see in her eyes that this was not a good thing.

Suddenly the skiff violently shifted direction. Neena had changed our course. Why? I looked back over my shoulder. Of course! We had been heading back toward the spot where I caught the salmon. This was the shortest route to the shore, but it was also where the deep water came right up against the rocks. If we continued in that direction, there would be no escape; the orcas would be able to follow us all the way to the shoreline. By veering off toward a different part of the shoreline, we would be heading to safety in the shallower waters, but the distance was quite a bit greater, giving the orcas more time to catch us. Looking back over Neena's shoulder, I could see that the orcas were not tiring; their dark, pointed dorsal fins were inching closer and starting to look menacing.

"They're still gaining!" I said grimly. It had probably been less than three minutes since we first spotted the killer whales, but I was already feeling exhausted by the ordeal and wondered how much longer I could hold onto the straining Lab. Perhaps Neena was wondering the same thing, because that moment was when she informed me of her plan: throw the dog in when she said so. Give the struggling, barking animal what he so desperately wanted. It was either going to be us or the dog. All of this for a salmon, I thought despondently. The salmon! Where was it? Looking around the skiff, I realized that Kenai was sitting on it: making a mess out of it really, with his doggy claws. Luckily, the tail was within close reach. Without really thinking or planning out what I was about to do, I leaned over and grabbed the tail and started pulling on it. At first nothing happened, then the dog shifted to catch his balance after being hit by a wave, and the fish popped free. In one motion I lifted the tail to the gunwale. Neena realized what I was about to do and shouted for me to stop. I don't think she wanted to save the salmon over the dog, but I am guessing she figured the dog was going to be a goner anyway, so why waste a valuable fish too? I ignored her. I didn't want to be responsible for tossing the dog into the sea. Somehow it seemed like a mortal sin to do this, even though the dog was doing his best to convince me otherwise. By lifting up my knee, I was able to brace the fish on my thigh, and with a boost from my leg and a yank over the edge of the boat that almost caused me to fall overboard, I dropped the fish into the water with a splash. I sat back down again, exhausted. I looked dully over Neena's shoulder, whose face had taken on a rather grim look, as if the day had gone from bad to worse. Were the orcas stopping for the fish? Would they all stop or just one, with the rest pressing on in hot pursuit? How can you tell when orcas are feeding? Is there a big feeding frenzy in one spot or do they just grab the fish and keep on going? The salmon was already dead, so there would not be any splashing or flailing of fins. At that point I only cared that I might have done something to potentially help our situation.

Again looking back at the killer whales, it seemed like they were still following but were not getting any closer. In fact, it seemed like they might be falling back a little.

"I think we are reaching shallower water," Neena said excitedly. I looked back over my shoulder and saw that the shoreline was much closer. I turned back forward just in time to see the orcas veer off toward the area where I had caught the salmon, perhaps having spotted its replacement or maybe because the area we were approaching had become too shallow for their liking.

"I think they are turning off," I said hopefully. Neena's facial expression turned from pensive concentration to relief. She kept up full speed until we neared the shore, then cut the engine. We drifted and searched for any sign of the orca. All was quiet except for the puffins skirting just above the gently slapping waves.

"We are going to have to go back the long way, around the island, to make sure we do not run into them again," she said. "We should have just enough gas."

We set out on our island circumnavigation. During the trip, we did not talk much. I was still sort of in a state of shock. Had this really happened or was it a dream? Were the killer whales really chasing us, or did they just happen to be going in the same direction? Would I really have tossed the dog overboard if Neena had given the word? I guess I will never know.

A few days later, when the bush pilot picked me up to go back to Cordova, he asked me if I liked Peak Island and did anything unusual happen. I looked at him and then looked out at the Sound.

"No, nothing unusual for Alaska, I guess."

Additional Readings

Anchorage Daily News article at http://www.adn.com/evos/evos.html.

Babcock, M. M., G. V. Irvine, P. M. Harris, J. A. Cusick, and S. D. Rice. 1996. Persistence of oiling in mussel beds three and four years after the *Exxon Valdez* oil spill. In *Proceedings of the* Exxon Valdez *Oil Spill Symposium,* ed. S. D. Rice, R. B. Spies, D. A. Wolfe, and B. A. Wright, 286–297. American Fisheries Society Symposium 18. Bethesda, MD: American Fisheries Society.

Johnson, S. W., M. G. Carls, R. P. Stone, C. C. Brodersen, and S. D. Rice. 1997. Reproductive success of Pacific herring (*Clupea pallasi*) in Prince William Sound, Alaska, six years after the *Exxon Valdez* oil spill. *Fishery Bulletin* 95:368–379.

Moles, A. 1998. Sensitivity of ten aquatic species to long-term crude oil exposure. *Bulletin of Environmental Contamination and Toxicology* 61:102–107.

Murphy, M. L., R. A. Heintz, J. W. Short, M. L. Larsen, and S. D. Rice. 1999. Recovery of pink salmon spawning after the *Exxon Valdez* oil spill. *Transactions of the American Fisheries Society* 128:909–918.

Peterson, C. H., S. D. Rice, J. W. Short, D. Esler, J. L. Bodkin, B. E. Ballachey, and D. B. Irons. 2003. Long-term ecosystem response to the *Exxon Valdez* oil spill. *Science* 302:2082–2086.

Rice, S. D., R. E. Thomas, R. A. Heintz, A. C. Wertheimer, M. L. Murphy, M. G. Carls, J. W. Short, and A. Moles. 2001. Impacts to pink salmon following the *Exxon Valdez* oil spill: Persistence, toxicity, sensitivity, and controversy. *Reviews in Fishery Science* 9 (3):165–211.

Short, J. W., and R. A. Heintz. 1997. Identification of *Exxon Valdez* oil in sediments and tissues from Prince William Sound and the Northwestern Gulf of Alaska based on PAH weathering. *Environmental Science and Technology* 31:2375–2384.

Hold That Pose Please

STANLEY TRAUTH

🕊 MY INTEREST IN color-slide photography grew out of a necessity to capture on film all stages of morphology, life history, and ecology of amphibians and reptiles. In 1980, early in my career as an academician, herpetologist, and field biologist, I agreed to participate with two colleagues in the writing of a book on Arkansas herpetology. This promise actually opened the door to a remarkably fascinating and personally rewarding adventure into organismal photography, which has now lasted for more than twenty-five years and continues to consume a large amount of my time. Rather than borrow color slides for this enormous task from several of my camera-proficient colleagues (or purchase one-time slide usage of slides from professional color-slide vendors), I decided to generate a set of color slides for all species by myself. The end product of this endeavor, the Arkansas herpetology book that was published by the University of Arkansas Press in 2004, has over 530 of my color photographs.

Becoming a dedicated outdoor photographer of amphibians and reptiles was never my true ambition or intention because I had already focused my academic career on becoming a proficient microscopic photographer. I have often used photomicrographs (both light as well as electron micrographs) in publications during my professional career as a vertebrate reproductive histologist.

I actually started dabbling into outdoor photography during a field study of collared lizards for my master's thesis during the early 1970s. At that time, a family friend purchased for me a Minolta SRT-101, a manual, single-lens, reflex (SLR) camera with a through-the-lens metering (TTL) system (a Minolta advancement), while he was visiting Germany in 1970.

As I recall, the price was a bargain at about two hundred dollars for the camera body and two lenses.

I knew nothing about SLR cameras as a beginning graduate student at the University of Arkansas at Fayetteville in 1971. A fellow graduate student there had kindly loaned me his then-antiquated SLR camera system that possessed a telephoto lens. I intended to use his photo equipment to take some long-distance photos of these lizards as they were perched upon rocks in cedar glades. In those days, most cameras were not fully automatic in terms of light metering, shutter speeds, etc. In fact, I can still recall my great frustration in trying to capture quality images of these lizards while attempting to simultaneously adjust numerous settings for an assortment of habitat conditions. For example, adjustments were necessary for changing sunlight conditions, film speed, and distance from the subject. Other variables to be determined included the proper F-stop, shutter speed, and flash setting. In the old "manual" SLR cameras, all of these settings were critical factors in the overall process of obtaining high-quality photographic images. I also remember failing miserably with his camera, and I was really looking forward to receiving my new Minolta. This newer SLR was supposed to be foolproof and, unfortunately for me (although I didn't know it at the time), possessed no flash capabilities. I hoped, however, that the new camera would allow me to gain some reasonable confidence in "shooting" live animals. I used this trusty manual Minolta camera for many years (had it repaired twice) for mostly habitat photos, but I eventually began to realize that my animal photographs were, at best, still of very marginal quality. I needed to advance my camera technology as well as my proficiency if I were to use my own color slides for a book.

It was not until I arrived at Arkansas State University in 1984 that I began to seriously investigate better camera systems and consider what the phrase "high-quality color slides" really meant. I liked my camera's manual control (operating modes) when taking photographs (and I remain inclined that way today). My manual Minolta camera system was much less expensive than the fully automatic SLRs that had begun flooding the market. In 1987, I finally decided to purchase a modestly priced system: a Minolta X-370s camera body, an attachable flash unit, and a high-quality macro lens. The macro lens by itself cost over $250! The most important improvement in my photography, however, was definitely having a SLR camera with a "hot shoe" for flash photography. And so began my pursuit of high-quality images. With this advanced system, I finally felt comfortable photographing animals and was able to perform some critical adjustments to remarkably improve my background lighting and depth-of-field photography.

Since 1987, I have gone through several manual camera bodies and flash units and have generated thousands of color slides over the many years of pursuing the "perfect photo image" of each animal. Today's highly advanced digital cameras and their technological interfacing with computers have basically rendered color-slide film photography obsolete, although I still retain a functional manual SLR system just in case I feel the urge to supplement my modern digital SLR camera. All photographs within the Arkansas herpetology book, however, were extracted from color-slide images.

My pursuit to capture quality images for the book actually took me in two directions. For one, I needed the standard, whole-organism, outdoor (and indoor) photos along with body close-up shots; but in addition, I decided to try my hand at aquarium photography in order to photograph various amphibian life stages: eggs and larvae. This photographic method required the building of aquaria of various sizes and shapes to match a given body size or egg cluster. I constructed three of these aquaria in 1988, and all are still in use. I also decided that for all of these images I would use direct sunlight instead of flash lighting. My setup for these photos was

Aquarium used to photograph larval amphibians.
PHOTOGRAPH BY STANLEY TRAUTH.

staged in the rear of my van (and eventually a Suburban). I spent endless hours coordinating sunlight and organism position for these close-up photos. For every egg mass or larval photograph in the book (about two hundred photos in all), I probably generated ten to fifteen additional photos of each that were not used. I utilized colorful backgrounds made of construction paper mounted on a wooden stand. The background effect worked quite well and provided a multitude of color possibilities for the aquaria. In addition, I tried to photograph a chronology of different life stages for these animals. Cloudy conditions and windy days were my nemeses in performing this type of photography. Yet, these larval photos probably represent my most prized achievement as a photographer.

Some of my most memorable field experiences are tied to specific photographs that appear in the Arkansas herpetology book. I normally carry my camera bag with me into as many habitats as possible because I never know exactly what type of photo opportunity I might have in the field. I always try to have the camera ready for any unexpected or unique situations. Besides the staged, indoor photographic sessions using captured animals, I have also photographed outside at all times of the day and night. I have photographed in caves and abandoned mine shafts, within rock quarries and rocky talus slides, on cedar glades, while wading in ponds and ditches or kneeling in spring heads, and standing in creeks and rivers.

Larval mole salamander (*Ambystoma talpoideum*)
in photographic aquarium.
PHOTOGRAPH BY STANLEY TRAUTH.

I almost had my camera and lenses bag stolen during a field trip to southern Texas in 1982. I was with some academic colleagues, and we had parked our vehicle under a bridge to escape the heat of the day near the Rio Grande River at Laredo. I left my camera inside our rental car during a brief collecting stint for lizards within the tall grasses that bordered the river. As I was walking down a sandy path, I was passed by a young boy speeding away on his bicycle. Moments later and upon returning to the car, my colleagues and I realized that the car's back windows had been shattered and my camera was missing. Not to be undone by this young thief, I realized that he wasn't carrying anything with him on the bicycle. A few minutes of diligent searching yielded the camera bag stuffed inside a drainage pipe about fifty meters from the vehicle. Even today, I'm still uneasy about leaving my camera in my vehicle during field trips (but see comments below).

The following are a few special glimpses into my photographic memory bank. I can recall in August 1991 crawling on my belly, camera in hand, about fifteen feet on a hot sandstone glade to photograph a pair of eastern collared lizards posed like miniature dinosaurs on the lichen-covered stone. As I inched toward the lizards, I frantically photographed them, hoping that they would not move. Fortunately for me, they were just as curious about me as I was about them. The ten to fifteen minutes

Female (*left*) and male (*right*) eastern collared lizards (*Crotaphytus collaris*) basking on a rock on a cedar glade.
PHOTOGRAPH BY STANLEY TRAUTH.

I spent maneuvering toward the lizards to capture a profile view of them was well worth the effort.

Another time I remember being alone in a small boat in the middle of Millwood Lake (in southwestern Arkansas) and being drenched with sweat and rain during a stormy summer night (July 1990). I paddled the boat along the shoreline looking for any frog or snake to photograph and finally came upon a female midland water snake resting on a stump. I gently eased the boat up to her so as not to frighten her away. To my surprise, she remained motionless, and I took a series of flash photos just inches from her.

One of my most prized (and, in fact, award-winning) photographs was taken at night in June of 1990. I must admit this series of photographs was totally serendipitous because I was not expecting to discover my very first bird-voiced treefrogs. A graduate student and I were looking for several species of toads and, just by chance, heard the distinct whistling mating calls of bird-voiced males. We carefully proceeded to wade into the waist-deep swampy water of Calion Lake in southern Arkansas and hap-

Female midland water snake (*Nerodia sipedon pleuralis*)
resting on a tree stump.
PHOTOGRAPH BY STANLEY TRAUTH.

Bird-voiced treefrogs (*Hyla avivoca*) photographed while in amplexus.
PHOTOGRAPH BY STANLEY TRAUTH.

pened upon a breeding pair of these frogs clutching a fallen tree branch sticking out of the water.

The discovery in March of 1996 of a western diamondback rattlesnake was quite a momentous adventure. An Arkansas State University colleague and I were visiting a specific locality in Perry County near the community of Aplin. I had visited this particularly rugged hillside many times in the past in an attempt to find rattlesnakes that had been reported to occur there by Marlin Perkins (former director of the St. Louis Zoo) back in 1928. We ventured out onto a sloping talus slide of rocks and, amazingly, found a large female rattlesnake basking at the mouth of her overwintering den site. On this occasion I had left my camera inside my vehicle to avoid dropping or breaking it during the strenuous trek over the rocky landscape. So, in order to photograph this western diamondback in its natural habitat, I had to swiftly walk back to my vehicle over a quarter of a mile away, retrieve my camera, and return back to the remote site through brush and briers to capture a ideal image of this serpent before it moved.

Western diamondback rattlesnake (*Crotalus atrox*) near its denning site.
PHOTOGRAPH BY STANLEY TRAUTH.

American alligators (*Alligator mississippiensis*) at the Little Rock Zoo.
PHOTOGRAPH BY STANLEY TRAUTH.

As I was nearing completion of almost all of the essential photographs for the book in July of 1999, there was still one major gap—I still had no shots of an American alligator. The best way to resolve this problem was to photograph a captive gator, and the Little Rock Zoo was just the place to go. Randal Berry, curator of reptiles at the zoo, allowed me access into the zoo's public display of caged alligators and also offered a bit of protection. With a broom in one hand and my camera in the other, I moved cautiously toward several of the docile six-footers. I was within ten feet of a pair when they started to hiss and become greatly disturbed by my presence. Fortunately, I didn't have to use the broom to defend myself and was very pleased to be able to photograph these ancient reptiles before any bloodletting—my blood—occurred.

Finding and photographing salamander eggs has always had a special lure for me. While scuba diving in the Eleven Point River in June of 2000, my graduate student (Ben Wheeler), a field companion (Vernon Hoffman), and I had a unique opportunity to examine an egg cluster of the Red River mudpuppy. Ben and Vernon pulled up a large rock from its sediment and uncovered an aggregate of sac-like eggs individually but firmly attached on the underside of the rock. I immediately grabbed my camera to take photographs of this salamander's eggs, which we had never seen before in the wild.

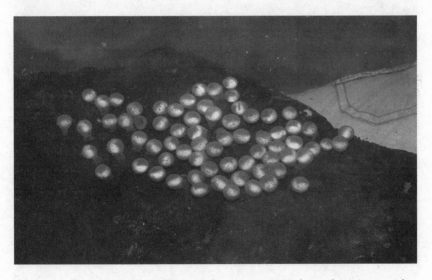

Eggs of the Red River mudpuppy (*Necturus maculosus louisianensis*).
PHOTOGRAPH BY STANLEY TRAUTH.

My recent field research has lured my graduate students and me into many unusual habitats. One such site was the inside an abandoned mine shaft in the Ouachita Mountains in order to study the egg-laying habits of a terrestrial salamander. The mine shaft, near Hot Springs, runs more than 450 feet straight into a mountainside. It just so happens that female western slimy salamanders utilize the walls of this mine from late summer to mid winter to lay their eggs; they remain with their eggs during the entire brooding process. What's even more interesting has been the fact that the same females will return to the mine year after year. By using our photographic records of all females that have entered the mine, we have been able to document nest-site fidelity in several individuals. One female, affectionately named "Four-spot" because of a spotting design on her rump, returned to the same nesting perch (336 feet from the mouth of the mine) to lay her eggs for five consecutive years!

Photography has been both a hobby and a vocation for me. I hope to always have a camera nearby in the field and in the lab. Capturing the eye of an organism or the morphology of a tissue is my "cup of tea" and allows me to preserve forever those many special moments.

Brooding female western slimy salamander (*Plethodon albagula*).
PHOTOGRAPH BY STANLEY TRAUTH.

Additional Readings

Trauth, S. E. 1989. Distributional survey of the eastern collared lizard, *Crotaphytus collaris collaris* (Squamata: Iguanidae), within the Arkansas River valley of Arkansas. *Proceedings of the Arkansas Academy of Science* 43:101–104.

Trauth, S. E., and B. G. Cochran. 1992. In search of western diamondback rattlesnakes (*Crotalus atrox*) in Arkansas. *Bulletin of the Chicago Herpetological Society* 27:89–94.

Trauth, S. E., M. L. McCallum, R. R. Jordan, and D. A. Saugey. 2006. Brooding postures and nest site fidelity in the western slimy salamander, *Plethodon albagula* (Caudata: Plethodontidae), from an abandoned mine shaft in Arkansas. *Herpetological Natural History* 9:141–149.

Trauth, S. E., W. E. Meshaka, and B. P. Butterfield. 1989. Reproduction and larval development in the marbled salamander, *Ambystoma opacum* (Caudata: Ambystomatidae), from Arkansas. *Proceedings of the Arkansas Academy of Science* 43:109–111.

Trauth, S. E., and J. W. Robinette. 1990. Notes on the distribution, mating activity, and reproduction in the bird-voiced treefrog, *Hyla avivoca*, in Arkansas. *Bulletin of the Chicago Herpetological Society* 25:218–219.

Trauth, S. E., H. W. Robison, and M. V. Plummer. 2004. *The amphibians and reptiles of Arkansas.* Fayetteville: University of Arkansas Press.

Walker, J. M., S. E. Trauth, J. M. Britton, and J. E. Cordes. 1986. Burrows of the parthenogenetic whiptail lizard *Cnemidophorus laredoensis* (Teiidae) in Webb Co., Texas. *Southwestern Naturalist* 31:408–410.

Rooting for New Medicines

FABRICIO MEDINA-BOLÍVAR

꿿 MANY YEARS AGO when I was doing my biology studies in a university in my native country, Peru, I realized that I wanted to do research with plants. Having been born in a country with an enormous culture in traditional medicine, I should not be astonished by the potential for the discovery of plants that can be used to treat major diseases such as cancers and AIDS. Any time one would go to an herbal market in Lima or in the countryside, one was always presented with a plant to treat any illness. After trips to the Amazon rainforest, it was not surprising to me that the incredible host of plant biodiversity in areas like that represents an unlimited reservoir of genetic and medicinal resources that still remain to be investigated.

I had the privileged opportunity right after I finished my bachelor studies to work at the prestigious International Potato Center (CIP) in Lima. Potatoes originated in Peru, and the CIP has acquired thousands of potato samples from all over the world. All of this material is kept in small glass test tubes—*in vitro*, via a technique called plant tissue culture. This technique allows plants to be maintained and grown in an artificial environment, not in the soil. My task at CIP was to develop a technique in tissue culture called organogenesis for the root crop sweetpotato, which, for clarification, is not a relative of white or red potatoes, which are tuber crops.

Organogenesis is the process of developing or "regenerating" new plants from any nonreproductive part of the plant—for example, to develop entire plants from a segment of a leaf. This process has many applications, and in those days we wanted to introduce novel genes into the newly regenerated plants in the process of genetic engineering. This research project was very challenging and exciting as well. I spent many hours in the laboratory experimenting with different plant hormones to find the right combination that would result in regeneration of a new plant—my research was more like an art form at the end. Fortunately, I was very successful, and after two years of working on this project, I developed many skills in tissue culture.

About that time I was contacted by researchers in the United States who were interested in my work. One of them was Dr. C. S. Prakash from Tuskegee University. He was also working with sweetpotato, and we published together my first peer-reviewed publication. Dr. Prakash was my link to coming to the United States; before that time I never thought of leaving my country or my family. After I mentioned to him my deep interest in medicinal plants, he put me in contact with Dr. Hector Flores, who was at Pennsylvania State University. Dr. Flores offered me an assistantship to conduct my PhD studies at Penn State, and thus I entered the world of medicinal plants. At Penn State I learned about a plant-tissue-culture technique called "hairy roots."

Dr. Flores was a pioneer in using hairy roots to study the production of specialized chemicals by plants, many of these with applications in medicine. This technique takes advantage of a soil bacterium, *Rhizobium rhizogenes* (formerly *Agrobacterium rhizogenes*), which is able to transfer part of its genetic material into the genetic code of plant cells to redirect them to produce roots—the so-called hairy roots. These roots can be grown in the laboratory in glass vessels without attached stems or leaves.

Because plants cannot move, they have evolved unique mechanisms to protect themselves from different environmental stresses and pathogens. They do so by producing a large number of complex chemicals that can, for example, act to stop the invasion of a pathogen into their tissues. In many cases these chemicals are only produced upon exposure of the plant to the pathogen, and for that reason it is difficult to find them when the plants are in a completely healthy environment. Interestingly, these pathogen-induced defense chemicals are the ones that have attracted most of my attention in the last years—these chemicals represent a valuable source of new medicines.

The hairy roots grown in their own glass containers exist in a controlled environment in which they can be induced to produce the unique chemicals that plants make in the wild in respond to pathogens. In the laboratory, we can reproduce these conditions by the use of "elicitors" (for more information see Flores and Medina-Bolivar [1995] and Guillon et al. [2006]). Elicitors are the signal compounds that plants recognize and to

Hairy roots of peanut can be induced to produce anti-cancer chemicals.
PHOTOGRAPH BY FABRICIO MEDINA-BOLÍVAR.

which they respond by producing self-defense chemicals. In many cases these could be as simple as heavy metals or any chemical that is foreign to the plant—for example, a compound from crab shells can induce production of these defense chemicals in the hairy roots.

During the five years of my doctoral studies, I did research with hairy roots of the Egyptian henbane—scientifically known as *Hyoscyamus muticus*. This plant is a member of the nightshade family, a group of plants that includes tobacco, potato, tomato, and chili pepper. The Egyptian henbane is a very interesting plant; it produces an important medicinal chemical in its roots called hyoscyamine. History tells us that Cleopatra used extracts from this plant to dilate her pupils—a symbol of beauty in antiquity. Interestingly, today these chemicals are used to dilate the pupil during an eye exam. Besides producing hyoscyamine, the hairy roots of this plant can be induced to produce defense chemicals that are secreted out of the roots into the liquid solution in which they are growing. Several years after my doctoral studies, I have come back to study these roots—but now with a new purpose. I am now searching for new anti-Parkinson's chemicals.

Toward the end of my doctoral studies, I realized that I needed to increase my skills in other areas of biotechnology; molecular biology was definitely a major area that I needed to strengthen. At the same time, I also wanted to learn how to turn research into a business—how to take chemicals out of the plant and turn them into commercial products. This was something that always attracted me, even back when I was in Peru. I had two great offers when I finished my PhD studies; one was to work at a prestigious natural-products center and the other was an offer from Virginia Tech to be a research scientist. I decided to go to Virginia Tech because of my interest in learning more about molecular biology and also because that position allowed me to be in close contact with the biotechnology and business community. That is where I met Dr. Carole Cramer. I worked in her laboratory and also did consultant work for her company—CropTech, a company that specializes in producing pharmaceutical proteins in tobacco. Working with her was a great experience and had a very positive impact on my professional career.

With my expertise in hairy roots and the training that I received in molecular biology, I engaged in a new application for the hairy-root technology. I began introducing novel genes into hairy roots to produce novel proteins, many of them with pharmaceutical applications. For example, the first demonstration of this application was a collaborative project at Dr. Cramer's laboratory where we developed hairy roots to produce "human protein C," an important blood protein with roles in the coagulation/anticoagulation pathway.

One of our major achievements while I was working with Dr. Cramer was to use tobacco hairy roots to produce a model delivery system for vaccines. We used a non-toxic lectin (a protein that binds to sugars) from castor bean to deliver protein antigens (these are the compounds that our immune system recognizes as foreign and tries to defend against). We manipulated the tobacco hairy roots to make this lectin and tested it as a deliver system in vaccine trials done with mice.

I learned a lot of immunology, and the interface of plant biotechnology with medicine was great. After working with Dr. Cramer for several years, I started my own research group; it was very nice to have my own lab and own projects—even in a small laboratory in one of the oldest buildings at Virginia Tech. Of course, my research continued to be on applications of hairy roots. I started with vaccine-related projects. We were using tobacco hairy roots to produce model vaccines for diseases such as pneumonic plague, periodontitis, and gonorrhea. I developed a very nice and productive research team—I feel very proud of them. While working on these projects, I was approached by a very well known scientist, Neal

Castagnoli Jr., who had heard about my expertise with tobacco and producing chemicals in tissue culture. His research was on understanding the correlation between tobacco smoking and a lower incidence of Parkinson's disease; he had identified some potential chemicals in tobacco smoke that could be responsible for this effect. However, as you might think, it was nearly impossible to extract a large amount of these chemicals out of the tobacco smoke. I came on board and we began using hairy roots to make these chemicals. This is still an area of my research, now in Arkansas.

While working in academia, two my colleagues, Maureen Dolan and Selester Bennett, and I ventured to start our own biotechnology company. We began Nature Diagnostics, Inc., which is still in Virginia, and recently we incorporated Nature West, Inc., in Arkansas to focus more on plant-made chemicals using the hairy-root technology along with other techniques. This has been an interesting journey—from my start in the basement of one of our houses to a nice laboratory in the Corporate Research Center at Virginia Tech, where we had many exiting projects.

Just a couple of years ago I was invited to tour the Arkansas Biosciences Institute at Arkansas State University, which at that time was still under construction, and one year later I moved from Virginia to Arkansas to be a part of this amazing research institute and of the Department of Biological Sciences. This institution has really allowed me to expand in the research areas that I always wanted to pursue, to work with plants and use the hairy-root technology for the discovery of potential new medicines. Very quickly I started new collaborations and engaged in new projects with scientists on and off campus—the entrepreneurial aspects of this institute were also very attractive.

One project that developed very quickly was a collaborative effort between my laboratory and Nature West, Inc. The objective of the project was to use the hairy-root technology to produce resveratrol, an interesting chemical that is receiving a lot of attention these days. Its anti-oxidant, anti-cancer, and anti-aging properties, among many others, make this chemical a very hot commodity. We were able to successfully produce this chemical using hairy roots of peanut. This project created many new opportunities, and I received many invitations to talk about these findings. I also established collaborations with other research institutions to further investigate the applications of these chemicals produced in the peanut cultures. Because we can manipulate the production of resveratrol and other bioactive chemicals in the peanut hairy roots, the potential to discover new chemicals with importance in medicine is tremendous—who would have thought that peanut hairy roots might be the source of new anti-cancer drugs.

The intriguing world of hairy roots has taken me to many different places. Throughout the years, I received many requests from people wanting to learn more about this technology. Six years ago, I was invited to teach this technology in a workshop in Greece. In 2006, my colleague Argelia Lorence and I had out first International Workshop on Hairy Roots. Over forty people from many different parts of the country and abroad showed interest and attended the workshop. The attendants had the opportunity to learn during the hands-on laboratory practices how to develop the hairy-roots cultures. It was very gratifying to see other people interested in my passion. I truly believe this to be a technology that can make a big difference in the development of major medicines in the future.

Additional Readings

Flores, H., and F. Medina-Bolívar. 1995. Root culture and plant natural products: "Unearthing" the hidden half of plant metabolism. *Plant Tissue Culture Biotechnology* 1:59–74.

Guillon, S., J. Tremouillaux-Guiller, P. Pati, M. Rideau, and P. Gantet. 2006. Hairy root research: Recent scenario and exciting prospects. *Current Opinion in Plant Biology* 9:1–6.

Medina-Bolívar, F., and C. Cramer. 2004. Production of recombinant proteins in hairy roots cultured in plastic sleeve bioreactors. In *Recombinant gene expression: Reviews and protocols*, ed. P. Balbas and A. Lorence, 351–363. Totowa, NJ: Humana Press.

Medina-Bolívar, F., and H. Flores. 1995. Selection for hyoscyamine and cinnamoyl putrescine overproduction in cell and root cultures of *Hyoscyamus muticus. Plant Physiology* 108:1553–1560.

———. 1998. Biosynthesis of constitutive versus inducible metabolites in hairy root cultures of *Hyoscyamus muticus*. In *Radical biology: Advances and perspectives on the function of plant roots*, ed. H. E. Flores, J. P. Lynch, and D. Eissenstat, 430–431. Rockville, MD: American Society of Plant Physiologists.

Medina-Bolívar, F., R. Wright, D. Sentz, L. Barroso, T. Wilkins, W. Petri Jr., and C. Cramer. 2003. A non-toxic lectin for mucosal antigen delivery of plant-based vaccines. *Vaccine* 21:997–1005.

Reed, D., L. Nopo-Olazabal, B. Woffenden, V. Funk, M. Reidy, C. Cramer, and F. Medina-Bolívar. 2004. Expression of functional hexahistidine-tagged ricin B in tobacco. *Plant Cell Reports* 24:15–24.

Search for the
Lost Pecos Gambusia

Adventures in the Land of Enchantment

JAMES BEDNARZ

❧ EVERYBODY WORKS HARD for that one big break that catapults one into his or her chosen vocation, really not knowing what to expect or even being certain if the "dream" job is truly the right match for one's interests and passions. Since grade school, I wanted to be a wildlife biologist in search of rare and difficult-to-find species and mysteries of nature —blazing a trail to discovery and saving the critical elements of nature. As a young lad, I pictured myself slogging through quicksand in a driving storm with lightning and thunder all about in search of that rare and elusive species in an effort to make a difference and, perhaps, to make the world a better place for all peoples.

At some point in my boyhood, I saw a documentary on endangered and extinct wildlife species. A portion of that documentary dealt with the final efforts to study and conserve the ivory-billed woodpecker (*Campelphilus principalis*) in the 1930s and 1940s. Still vivid in my memory, a film segment in that documentary showed researchers from the Cornell Lab of Ornithology slogging through the bayous and bottomlands in Louisiana, pushing and pulling an ox-drawn wagon with state-of-the-art recording equipment (for the mid 1930s) in an effort to find and record an ivory-billed woodpecker. As the wagon was dragged through a deep mud hole in the swamp, one man (whom I later identified as Jim Tanner) was mud-covered and pushing the wagon from behind. I thought to myself, "That is what I want to do for a living." I wanted to be that go-to guy pushing the wagon against all adversities in an effort to save the last of a dying species for all mankind. Little did I know when I had that dream that I, indeed, would have an opportunity to slog through the mud in search of the king of woodpeckers nearly forty years later, but that is another story.

My initial challenge was determining how to begin a career slogging through swamps after rare species and make a living at it. This is the story of how I started my career as a biologist, trudging through the muck in search of the holy grails of the biological world.

I started my career preparation by majoring in fisheries and wildlife biology at New Mexico State University and carefully heeded the advice given to me by my professors and fellow students that getting those first jobs in wildlife or biology in order to gain valuable experience was critical to ultimately having a successful career in the field of natural resource conservation. In that effort, I worked one summer at a ring-necked pheasant (*Phasianus colchicus*) farm, which produced birds for harvest, and I became a research intern at Argonne National Laboratory on a project to evaluate the biological integrity of newly emerging computer-simulation models for aquatic ecosystems.

As I always enjoyed physical work, I appreciated that outdoor experience and opportunity to work with animals at the pheasant farm. But this experience fell far short of exploring the uncharted wilds for a rare wildlife species. I also worked many hours at the computer-ecosystem-simulation-assessment position, spending many long evenings running computer models, examining output, and analyzing that output to determine how it might reflect reality. However, I often had trouble concentrating on the reams of computer output and tended to stare outside, feeling that I really needed to be outside experiencing nature instead of trying to simulate it. I made up my mind that computer modeling was OK for some, but definitely not right for me—I needed a job in the field!

The Break

I received a newspaper article about the brand-new Endangered Species Program of the New Mexico Department of Game and Fish and the efforts of new director, Dr. John P. Hubbard, to get the program off the ground. I wrote a very carefully worded letter describing my interests in working with endangered species and summarized my experiences as a biologist to date. The timing of my letter was perfect, as my correspondence landed on Dr. Hubbard's desk just as he was trying to allocate his limited but brand-new research budget to maximize efforts to assess the status of numerous species listed as threatened or endangered in the state of New Mexico, the Land of Enchantment.

Dr. Hubbard's primary expertise was in birds, but he had the responsibility to conserve all species, including numerous fish and other aquatic species. My three and a half years of academic training in fisheries and limited experience working on the research of aquatic systems seemed to make me a good match, in Dr. Hubbard's assessment, for a summer position studying the current status of the Pecos gambusia (*Gambusia nobilis*). This was a small mosquitofish that varied between a half inch and two inches in length and was endemic to eastern New Mexico and parts of Texas and was classified as endangered. This fish had been reported from several localities in eastern New Mexico over the years, but many of these records were old, and nobody could vouch for the current status of the Pecos gambusia in the Land of Enchantment as I undertook my summer job with the New Mexico Department of Game and Fish. My task was to search for, to find, and to assess the current status of the rare and endangered Pecos gambusia in the state of New Mexico—my dream job!

The Search Begins!

The New Mexico Department of Game and Fish provided me an old, two-wheel-drive pickup truck and gave me a purchase-order book to use to buy some limited research supplies. John Hubbard added some guidance and words of wisdom and had me contact a couple of the state's more prominent ichthyologists (specialists in fish biology) concerning my search for the Pecos gambusia. On my way down to southeastern New Mexico, the land of the Pecos gambusia, I stopped in Albuquerque and visited with Dr. William Koster, the recently retired ichthyologist at the University of New Mexico. Dr. Koster shared his observations of the species with me and showed me several Pecos gambusia specimens that were preserved in the ichthyology collection at the University of New Mexico.

After my introduction to Pecos gambusia preserved in formalin, I was off to Roswell, a town in southeastern New Mexico located just north of the reported range of my target species. Over the years, Roswell had gained some notoriety as the location of the infamous crash of an alien flying saucer in July 1947, an event often referred to as the "Roswell Incident." After an initial newspaper report briefly described the crash of a flying disk recovered by the U.S. Army, the story was almost immediately retracted, and the debris found in the New Mexico desert was identified subsequently by the U.S. military as an experimental weather balloon. When I headed to Roswell on June 3, 1975, this mysterious event was mostly forgotten; however, interest in the incident was revived in the

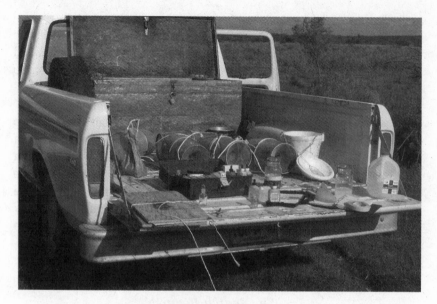

My summer equipment: an old truck, minnow traps, and nets.
PHOTOGRAPH BY JAMES BEDNARZ.

late 1970s after several eye witnesses to the original incident decided to comment publicly. Although the Roswell Incident is well known today in the town of Roswell and by UFO enthusiasts around the world, this incident was never mentioned during the entire summer I spent searching for the Pecos gambusia in 1975.

One of my initial challenges was to find a Pecos gambusia. This task was complicated by the fact that the Pecos gambusia appears very similar to the common mosquitofish (*Gambusia affinis*) that is very widespread and abundant throughout the range of the Pecos gambusia. Originally, the common mosquitofish was native to southeastern New Mexico as was the Pecos gambusia, but aggressive introduction programs of non-native varieties of common mosquitofish to control mosquitoes further increased the numbers and distribution of this common species.

Although I studied museum specimens of both species before I undertook my research in the Roswell area, fish stored in formalin or alcohol lose their color and appear considerably different than live fish. Complicating the identification challenge further was that many of the characteristics used to distinguish these two species involve color or pigmentation. In life, the Pecos gambusia is more heavily pigmented and more brightly colored than the common mosquitofish. Also, the Pecos gambusia does have a more distinctly arched back than the common mosquitofish and some reported differences in the number of rays in certain fins, but there is a lot of variation in both of these characteristics in both species. Furthermore, a description such as having a "greater arch" in the back is a rather subjective characteristic, so reading about this trait and recognizing it on fish in the field can be two different matters. To make my job even more difficult, hybrids between the two species have been reported with intermediate characteristics.

However, the search was on, and as is the case for any researcher of rare species, I felt that I was under rather intense pressure to succeed in finding my target species. I purchased minnow traps and dip nets and diligently lined them with nylon-tulle because the mesh in most nets and traps is too large to trap the small mosquitofish. I started my search at Bottomless Lakes State Park south of Roswell. At least one historical population of Pecos gambusia was reported in the state park. I searched the "bottomless" lakes, which were really sinkholes filled with water, in the state park and found several spring-fed ponds where I began my sampling. I found thousands and thousands—well, actually, hundreds of thousands of mosquitofish! Most looked like classic common mosquitofish: not too much pigment and their backs were slightly to moderately arched. But some individuals had darker pigment, a darker lateral line, more dark spots, and relatively more arch in their backs. I collected a few and examined them closely in the laboratory, counted fin rays and scales under a microscope, scratched my head, and re-counted the fin rays and scales until late in the night. The fin-ray counts were also confusing since there was tremendous variation; some approximated the criteria for identifying Pecos gambusia, and some were way off. The more subjective characteristics (such as pigment, coloration, and curvature of the back) seemed to vary randomly with the fin-ray counts.

I quickly learned that slogging through the mud and facing the elements in search of the rare Pecos gambusia was not the only obstacle that I would face. An even more significant challenge was the "simple" problem of identifying my target species in the face of massive numbers of the "look-alike" species, the common mosquitofish, which seemed to inhabit every puddle, lake, stream, and spring seep in southeastern New Mexico.

For days I continued my routine; I sampled with nets and minnow traps every pond, spring, or body of water I could find, sight-identifying most fish as "probably" the common mosquitofish. Occasionally, I would capture a few more-darkly pigmented fish (suspected Pecos gambusia?) and would collect a couple of voucher specimens.

In the evening, I would head to a small lab I set up at the Dexter National Fish Hatchery and thoroughly examine the specimens under a dissecting microscope. I poured over the identification keys and guides, re-counted and re-counted fin rays and scales, drew sketches, and pondered if I had encountered and collected specimens of a real Pecos gambusia. I classified most of these fish as "probable" common mosquitofish, and some I classified as "possible" Pecos gambusia. Or were they hybrids? Was it possible that the Pecos gambusia was gone from southeastern New Mexico and there only remained a few hybrids mixed within the abundant populations of the common mosquitofish that were everywhere? Had I already failed in my quest to find the rare and endangered Pecos gambusia?

More Problems!

One of the more promising reported localities of the Pecos gambusia was a series of sinkholes and spring seeps located at Bitter Lake National Wildlife Refuge. This refuge was operated by the federal agency, the U.S. Fish and Wildlife Service, which had a number of regulations in place to protect fish and wildlife resources. My position was with the state agency responsible for fish and wildlife resources, the New Mexico Department of Game and Fish, and therefore I had to abide by all the federal regulations protecting fish and wildlife on the refuge. The U.S. Fish and Wildlife staff was extremely helpful in facilitating my work, and I was given open access to all the closed portions of the refuge to sample for fish.

However, the decision was handed down that I could not collect any Pecos gambusia, even voucher specimens, from the refuge. This was a blow to my plans as it is common practice to collect a few voucher specimens from even endangered populations to verify the identification of the species examined in scientific investigations. The refuge staff did allow me to net and trap other fish, but if I captured a suspected Pecos gambusia, the fish had to be released immediately. As I was having difficulty identifying gambusia to a specific species even after measuring every dimension and counting every fin ray and scale in the lab, how could I sight-identify gambusia on the refuge to document their current distribution? Challenge upon challenge—it seemed as though I was sure to fail in my quest to find the Pecos gambusia.

Success Finally!

I continued my routine day in and day out, weekdays and weekends, sampling in the day and toiling in the lab at night. But I loved the field; yes, I was slogging through the mud in waders, netting and examining fish. Between ponds and spring seeps, I saw all sorts of wildlife that I had never before seen. Every species of bird, reptile, or mammal that I encountered, I stopped briefly to study and identify. It was almost as much fun and filled with as much excitement as I had imagined, except for the fact that I had yet to make certain identification of the Pecos gambusia—my primary mission. I didn't mind that lab work, and although it was frustrating because the characteristics and counts were all inconsistent with the literature and identification keys, I felt that sooner or later I would make a breakthrough; I just had to keep working.

Although I had only spent about twelve days searching for the elusive fish with no definitive verification that Pecos gambusia still existed in New Mexico, it felt like an eternity of failure. My first real breakthrough occurred at Blue Spring, located about five miles east of Whites City in Eddy County, New Mexico. Blue Spring was a reported historical locality for the Pecos gambusia and was on a private ranch. I found the rancher and asked him for permission to sample from Blue Spring on his property. He was interested in wildlife and was quite accommodating; he gave me complete access to the entire two-mile length of Blue Spring. Blue Spring was reported to have a large population of the common mosquitofish as well as the Pecos gambusia. With some trepidation, I started to survey the spring run, cautiously driving the rough two-track path that coarsely paralleled the length of the spring run. I wondered if I would again have the difficulty that I had during the last two weeks discriminating between the two species of mosquitofish. I still was not sure if I had seen any Pecos gambusia, and I was not very confident in my ability to distinguish the two species.

As this was private ground and I had a state permit to collect fishes, including the endangered Pecos gambusia, I could actively sample with nets and traps and collect voucher specimens as needed. I began my sampling in a relatively large marshy area off the main spring run, slogging around in my boots with dip nets and minnow traps in hand. Within minutes, I pulled my first sample of fish, and it included numerous gambusia fish. Many of these were different from the thousands of fish I had caught before—they were darker; they had a conspicuous black lateral line and many more pigmented spots; parts of the fish were colored "brilliant orange," and their backs were significantly arched! These "brilliant" gambusia were mixed in with a few of the much duller gambusia that were very similar to all previous fish I had captured! Hallelujah! Yes, I had finally found the Pecos gambusia—there was no doubt! The differences in all the characteristics over which I had sweated and pondered during the past two weeks were hugely obvious in live wild fish. Prior to seeing the Blue Spring fish, I was trying to convince myself that common mosquitofish with subtle differences were Pecos gambusia. I collected a voucher sample of both the Pecos gambusia and the common mosquitofish from Blue Spring.

I continued my sampling at Blue Spring for two days; in some localities I found the Pecos gambusia fairly abundant and mixed with a few common mosquitofish. In other locations in the spring run, I only found thousands of common mosquitofish and no sign of Pecos gambusia. An important research question emerged: Why were Pecos gambusia found in some locations in the same spring run and not others? Conversely, what factors dictated the distribution of the common mosquitofish, a potential competitor and harmful species to the Pecos gambusia, in the same waterway?

After I left Blue Spring, I raced back to the lab and compared all my newly acquired voucher specimens to the many gambusia I had collected previously. As I suspected, there were clear and distinctive differences between my Pecos gambusia sample from Blue Spring and all the other gambusia—the other voucher specimens that I had collected previously were all common mosquitofish.

I worked late into the night counting fin rays and scales on my new set of definite Pecos gambusia and found tremendous variation in the counts. The literature and identification keys were wrong! The counts of scales and fin rays, in fact, were very misleading. Both species showed incredible variation in these characteristics. At least based on my one Blue Spring sample, coloration and body shape were far more accurate characteristics by which to distinguish the two species than the numeric characteristics given in some of the identification keys.

These characteristics were easiest to distinguish when the fishes were alive and in their natural habitat. In fact, as soon as I netted or captured a Pecos gambusia, its natural colors began to fade, making identification more difficult. Pecos gambusia museum specimens stored in alcohol or formalin typically lose their color and are much more difficult to distinguish from common mosquitofish specimens stored in the same manner. The arched back is a good, but not easily quantifiable, characteristic. The micro-morphology of the male's anal fin (or gonopodium), which is specially modified to inseminate the female, is quantifiably and clearly distinguishable between the two species of mosquitofish. Thus, I could always clearly differentiate the species of collected male specimens by examining their gonopodia under a microscope. A drawing of the gonopodium characteristics of the Pecos gambusia, common mosquitofish, and a hybrid can be found in my article published in *Southwestern Naturalist* in 1979.

The Search Continues

My discovery at Blue Spring that Pecos gambusia can be clearly distinguished from the common mosquitofish by coloration in their natural habitat provided me with a new survey alternative at Bitter Lake National Wildlife Refuge. Standard sampling for small fishes involves using minnow traps and nets, examining and collecting the fish, and releasing individuals not used for voucher or study specimens. I was allowed to net and capture fish at Bitter Lake National Wildlife Refuge as long as I released all the suspected Pecos gambusia unharmed. I tried this approach, but it was very slow going. I only had a limited number of minnow traps and could only effectively sample a few sinkholes or water bodies over a week's time, repeatedly returning to check the traps, identifying and releasing the fish. There were nearly a hundred sinks, springs, spring seeps, and lakes at Bitter Lake National Wildlife Refuge. Using traditional sampling techniques, I could only sample a fraction of all the water on the refuge by the end of my summer work term.

Typical sinkhole at Bitter Lake National Wildlife Refuge.
PHOTOGRAPH BY JAMES BEDNARZ.

As I considered this next challenge, while I watched gambusia swim around a sinkhole at Bitter Lake and avoid my minnow trap, I realized that the water was quite clear in most of these sites. Also, I was an active competitive swimmer at New Mexico State University, certified scuba diver, and experienced snorkeler. Why not try a swimming survey! I donned my snorkel, mask, and fins the next day and dove in the next sinkhole on my list to survey, not sure how the fish would react to my presence. If they swam away and hid in the cover, then swim surveys would be ineffective. Amazingly, the fish showed little fear to this new giant creature in the water. The water was clear in most sinks and springs and the color characteristics of the Pecos gambusia were clearly obvious when the fish were swimming in their natural environment. In less than twenty minutes, I felt that I thoroughly surveyed all the small fishes in the entire sinkhole. I circled the perimeter of the sink near the surface and easily identified all the fish. Then I dove deep and circled the perimeter of the sink near the bottom. As opposed to using minnow traps that may have enabled me to sample a few hundred fish over the course of several days, with mask and snorkel I could quickly examine thousands of swimming fish in a matter of minutes. I even returned to sinks that I had previously sampled with minnow traps and recorded species that were never caught in traps and were previously unrecorded for that habitat. The mask-and-snorkel technique was incredibly efficient and effective compared to traditional techniques! I even took a hand counter with me later in the summer and felt I could obtain an accurate count of all the Pecos gambusia inhabiting a given sinkhole. Repeat counts were typically within 5 percent of each other.

What at first was a huge obstacle, the restriction not to collect at the refuge, actually stimulated me to develop an innovative approach to sampling Pecos gambusia and other small fishes that was far more efficient and superior to conventional techniques. By the end of my summer job, I felt I had thoroughly documented the distribution of the Pecos gambusia at Bitter Lake National Wildlife Refuge. I had identified seven discrete populations of Pecos gambusia on the refuge and obtained accurate estimates of population size for most of those habitats.

The Mystery of Dragonfly Spring

During my search for the Pecos gambusia, I made an effort to locate and assess the status of the species at all locations where it had previously been reported. One location reported by a past researcher was a site called

Snorkeling to survey for the Pecos gambusia.
PHOTOGRAPH BY JOHN E. MACCROSSEN.

Dragonfly Spring at Bitter Lake National Wildlife Refuge. The publication stated that Dragonfly Spring was approximately 75 meters (250 feet) southwest of the mouth of Lost River. Lost River was clearly identified on refuge maps, but Dragonfly Spring was not indicated and the refuge staff at the time was unaware of any site called Dragonfly Spring. Lost River was a small spring run that extended about 1,150 feet in length and emptied into an extremely shallow and saline mud flat called Sago Lake that was commonly used by shorebirds.

Lost River was a crystal-clear spring run that was inhabited by Pecos gambusia, but the water quality became extremely saline at the point where the spring emptied into Sago Lake. The only fish that apparently inhabited Sago Lake was the Pecos pupfish (*Cyrindon pecosensis*), which is a species extremely tolerant of saline conditions. Using my compass, I sighted due southwest (225 degrees) from the mouth of Lost River and estimated a distance of 250 feet. That location was in the middle of Sago Lake! This seemed odd to me, but I surmised that maybe there was a spring seep feeding the central portion of Sago Lake with adequate water quality to support the Pecos gambusia. It seemed to be a simple enough task to put on my waders and slog 250 feet through the muck and look for some swimming gambusia.

I put on my waders and began my trek to the middle of Sago Lake. The going immediately became a little "sticky." The substrate of the saline

Sago Lake was extremely soft. I first walked over the dry mudflat, but it became softer and softer as I approached the edge of the water. The water was extremely shallow (less than a half inch), yet my boots were sinking in the substrate up to my shins. The going was extremely difficult as I had to struggle to pull out each foot and boot from the mucky substrate one small step at a time.

After battling with the muck for maybe 35 feet into the lake, even though the water was only about an inch deep, my boots were sinking up to my knees. Each step required an extreme effort and took me minutes to execute, and with each step I sank further into the substrate. I soon realized that my boots were useless, and attempting to remain vertical had now caused me to sink up to my thighs in the muck, while the water was still only an inch or two deep. The water soon overflowed my waders, and I had to flop over to a horizontal position in order to pull me and my boots out of the mush of Sago Lake. I had, perhaps, progressed 70 feet toward my objective (180 feet to go), and I seemed to be hopelessly stuck in the mud.

It was time to cut my losses, retreat, and develop a new strategy to get to Dragonfly Spring. I went back to the original publication and reread carefully every word—there was no mistaking the description of the location of Dragonfly Spring, "approximately 75 meters southwest of the mouth of Lost River."

I realized I could not walk on the muck; I was sinking much too deep to even move. Thus, I reasoned that if I stayed horizontal, maybe I could "swim" or "crawl" on the shallow layer of surface water and make it out 250 feet to Dragonfly Spring. As a competitive swimmer (swimming as much as 10,000 meters a day during the season) and certified scuba diver, I was very confident in my skills in the water and felt that I could "swim through the muck."

The next day I decided not to bring any equipment with me, but just make the journey to Dragonfly Spring in the middle of Sago Lake. I would cross the bridge of getting any needed equipment (e.g., mask and snorkel) to the site after I figured how to get me there. This time, I only wore my swim suit. I started my walk to the edge of Sago Lake and again sank up to my ankles. After progressing about 35 feet into the lake, I was already sinking up to my knees. At least this time I did not have to exhaust myself pulling my boots as well as my feet out of the soft mud. Time to go horizontal—the water was only about an inch deep and was extremely warm (greater than 100 degrees F). My body "floated" reasonably well on the thin layer of surface water and underlying muck. I slowly began my swim, or, perhaps more aptly, crawl, on the mud to the middle of the lake. The water was so shallow that I could not avoid my hands, arms, and feet sinking into the muck, but I made slow progress.

Perhaps you can imagine someone trying to swim in Jell-O; however, this "Jell-O" was gritty, yucky, and stinky. The smell of rotten eggs (hydrogen sulfide) was all around. After traversing at least 150 feet (100 feet to go), I had found no sign of the clean, cool, freshwater Dragonfly Spring that I had imagined seeping up in the middle of the lake. The substrate was excessively soft, and even though I was attempting to float/swim/crawl on top of the surface water, I was sinking deeper and deeper into the mucky substrate. My arms were stuck up to my elbows, and my feet and ankles were caught under the muck as well. When I tried to raise my arm out of the muck, that action forced my body and head deeper into the water and muck soup to the point that I was not sure I could keep my mouth above the water, which was still only three inches or so deep.

If the water had been deeper I could have swum on the surface and could have completely avoided the mushy substrate. However, I needed close to twelve inches of surface water to swim above the mucky bottom. I had heard that there was no such thing as quicksand, but at that point every time I moved, the muck sucked me in deeper. If there was such a thing as quicksand—I thought I might have found it! At that point, I decided it was time to punt on finding Dragonfly Spring, at least for that day.

I slowly turned and swam/floated/crawled back to the edge of Sago Lake, which took at least fifteen minutes. I must have made it at least 200 feet (just 50 feet short) across the lake, but I had found no sign of the spring. How did those other guys get to Dragonfly Spring to sample fish? There was not one mention about the muck and the "quicksand" surrounding Dragonfly Spring in the original publication. I needed a new plan. If I could just make it a little bit further, I would be able to swim in the cool, clean, spring water.

Over the next few days, I formulated a new strategy to reach Dragonfly Spring. I called one of my swimming buddies, John E. MacCrossen, and asked him if he could help me get to a difficult-to-reach spring site in the middle of mud-flat lake. John was an excellent swimmer and was built like a body builder with extreme muscle definition; his body looked like that of Arnold Schwarzenegger in his prime. John was also solid and dependable, and we had been in more than one tight situation in collegiate competition and otherwise; I knew that I could always depend on John. Our modified plan included a safety rope tied around my waist with

John at the other end. If I started to sink in the quicksand of Sago Lake during my quest to reach Dragonfly Spring, it would be John's job to pull me out.

I purchased 300 feet of rope, which should have been more than adequate to extend the estimated 250-foot distance to Dragonfly Spring. I tied the rope securely around my waist and John did likewise; he did not plan on losing me no matter what happened. As John carefully coiled the rope while standing on the edge of Sago Lake in a location where the soil was firm, I took a compass bearing at 225 degrees, sighted a directional landmark, gradually slid into my horizontal position in the shallow water and muck, and began to "cruise" along the surface toward the reported location of Dragonfly Spring. I made steady progress, as I was now accustomed to lying in the muck with a thin layer of water and swimming/crawling over the surface of Sago Lake.

I glanced over my shoulder to see John E. solidly planted on the edge of the lake, gradually feeding out the rope to match my progress, with his biceps and triceps bulging out of his tank top. John looked like the consummate California lifeguard with his bleached blond hair and rippling muscles glistening in the desert sunlight. I ventured forth with new confidence that I was in secure hands if the quicksand tried to suck me into Sago Lake.

Soon I had crawled/swum past the farthest point of my previous attempts and reached what I estimated was the 250-foot distance from the mouth of Lost River. The water now may have exceeded three inches in depth, but the substrate was as soft as ever, and my hands, arms, and legs were covered in muck. I again glanced back at John E. and saw that he was firmly in the ready position to heave me out of the quicksand, with legs bent, muscles flexed, and hands and arms firmly grasping the last couple of feet of rope; this gave me another boost of confidence to continue on.

However, John was nearly out of rope, and I had not reached anything that hinted at being a spring seep into Sago Lake. I was still sloshing around in the thick stinking muck, fighting to keep my head above the shallow water. Maybe the previous researchers had underestimated the distance, and the spring was just a little farther and I was almost there? I had to proceed onward!

I motioned to John to move into the edge of Sago Lake; I knew the substrate at the edge was somewhat soft but relatively firm compared to the mush through which I was struggling near the center of the lake. John inched into the edge of the water and slowly sank deeper into the muck. I struggled onward into the middle of Sago Lake. The water was slightly deeper and the muck sucked my arms and legs to the bottom of the shallow lake. I must have proceeded over 300 feet from my point of origination and still there was no sign of the cool, clear spring water. I was still in thick, soft, smelly muck!

The muck started to encroach on my shoulders and back, pulling me deeper into Sago Lake, and I had to struggle to keep my mouth above the shallow water. It was time to give John E. the signal to haul me out of this mess. I was now convinced that there was no spring in the middle of Sago Lake. As I struggled and the muck sucked me deeper, I hollered to John E., "OK, pull me out!" Since John had inched several yards into the lake to give me enough slack to make it further toward the middle, I could see he was already in mud up to his knees. But on command, John E. gave a mighty heave, and I felt the rope tighten around my waist. In one clean, swift motion, John E. disappeared into the muck at the perimeter of the lake. Instead of pulling me out of the muck, he had pulled himself up to his neck into the sticky, smelly mess. At that point, while I struggled for air, I actually had to laugh at the way John E. had so quickly disappeared into the muck. I also realized that I was on my own and turned and slowly and carefully began swimming/crawling through the muck back to shore. I saw John E. struggling in the muck, trying to keep from getting sucked in further. At this point, I perhaps had an advantage over my friend because I had already spent several hours navigating through the muck during my previous attempts to reach Dragonfly Spring and was somewhat used to the sensation of being mostly buried while I maneuvered in the muck. By the time I had made considerable progress toward shore, I saw that John finally had his situation under control and had reached a little firmer ground. We were both covered with mud from head to toe and actually had a good laugh when we dragged our weary bodies onto dry ground.

Although I had already begun to suspect something was "amuck," my last attempt to reach the reported location of Dragonfly Spring with John E. MacCrossen's assistance convinced me that something was in error with the directions to Dragonfly Spring. After looking at the map and considering options, I paced 250 feet to the southeast, a direction that took me away from Sago Lake. Sure enough, as I climbed over a small sandy dune that obscured the lush low growth of vegetation, I found a small series of spring-fed marshy ponds that fed into Lost River. These spring ponds supported a good number of Pecos gambusia—this was the reported Dragonfly Spring.

Certainly, an important lesson that I learned during this first independent research project was that the published, peer-reviewed literature was not always infallible. In this case, a simple typo "southwest," instead of the correct direction "southeast," forced me to consume a lot of time and energy looking for an erroneous location, not to mention that it got John E. MacCrossen and me covered in muck—an experience that I will never forget.

Conclusion

I finished up my field work on the Pecos gambusia on September 1, 1975. I found eight populations of this rare fish and developed estimates of their numbers at each site. I also documented that the fish was extirpated from at least one location where it previously had occurred. I collected data on the ecological interactions of Pecos gambusia and the common mosquitofish and data on the range of aquatic habitat parameters correlated with the presence of this endangered species. I completed a report to the New Mexico Department of Game and Fish documenting all of my findings and later published a portion of that report in a peer-reviewed journal (Bednarz 1979) when I was in graduate school.

I learned many important lessons as a young undergraduate researcher during that project, including that you cannot always trust what you read even in a peer-reviewed scientific journal. Importantly, scientists should always question and verify, be open to new and innovative approaches, and review the data before drawing conclusions. Equally important is that I had a lot of fun, a great learning experience, and a number of rather fantastic adventures.

Dr. John Hubbard was pleased with my success in my search to find and to learn about the endangered Pecos gambusia. The following summer he hired me to search for and study the elusive and endangered white-sided jackrabbit (*Lepus callotis gallardi*) in southwestern New Mexico. I have been searching for rare species of conservation concern, making cool discoveries, and working hard for their conservation ever since, often slogging through the mud, dodging lightning storms, getting stuck in "quicksand," and having one great adventure after another, all in an effort to help conserve the world's biodiversity.

Additional Readings

Bednarz, J. C. 1979. Ecology and status of the Pecos gambusia, *Gambusia nobilis* (Poeciliidae), in New Mexico. *Southwestern Naturalist* 24:311–322.

Echelle, A. F., A. A. Echelle, and D. R. Edds. 1989. Conservation genetics of a spring-dwelling desert fish, the Pecos gambusia (*Gambusia nobilis,* Poeciliidae). *Conservation Biology* 3:159–169.

Thanksgiving Dinner with Memories of the Ozarks

Lightning, Persimmons, and Flies

TANJA MCKAY

THANKSGIVING HOLIDAY is a time to celebrate with family and friends a bountiful harvest and the pleasures of life. It is also a time to honor our pioneering ancestors and to sit down to a delicious turkey dinner with all the trimmings. In preparing for this meal, it usually takes a lot of organization, from planning the guest list and menu to preparing the meal. As we sit down to this fabulous feast, we give a toast, give thanks, and begin to eat our food. We seldom give thanks to the turkey, and most of us rarely give the source of the bird a second thought before devouring our meal. I, however, look at poultry in a different light. When I sit down to a roast turkey dinner, I have flashbacks of my summer of 2003, when I was introduced to persimmons, the rolling hills of the Ozarks, and dusty poultry houses.

It was my first year as a research associate in the Department of Entomology at the University of Arkansas. I spent that humid and hot summer traveling around the Arkansas countryside visiting turkey- and chicken-production facilities. My boss, Dayton Steelman, and I conducted research to evaluate various fly-control methods, such as parasitic wasps that are commonly used as biological control agents in the broiler-breeder and egg facilities. We also identified pathogens of food-quality importance such as *Campylobacter, Salmonella,* and *Escherichia coli* that are commonly harbored by flies.

In order to protect ourselves and to prevent the spread of disease from facility to facility, we dressed in white protective suits, hairnets, respirators, and plastic booties before entering these facilities. Since the turkeys

Sticky strips used to collect flies in poultry houses. *Left:* Fly strips from a facility with no fly problems. *Right:* Fly strips from a facility with a serious fly problem.

PHOTOGRAPH BY TANJA MCKAY

Spalangia cameroni (Hymenoptera: Pteromalidae), a parasitic wasp of houseflies.

PHOTOGRAPH BY TANJA MCKAY.

Young turkeys in a turkey finishing house.
PHOTOGRAPH BY TANJA MCKAY.

and chickens were also pure white, we were well camouflaged. In the broiler-breeder houses, the roosters often chased us with their spurs as though we were invaders of their territory. I am sure they perceived us as oversized roosters, there to steal away their harems. On a few occasions, their spurs tore through my protective suit. In the turkey-finishing houses, the toms grew so large that their heads were sometimes at chest height. We had to be careful when working around large birds since they would sometimes fly upwards. On those occasions, I would warn those turkeys that I was planning my Thanksgiving menu: and one of them was on my list. Fortunately, neither of us was ever seriously injured.

There was one occasion, however, when I thought I was on my way to being part of an early Thanksgiving dinner myself. We had just arrived at a turkey-finishing house when the skies opened up, and it began to pour. The dark clouds were very low and seemed to envelop the turkey house. Trying to keep from getting too wet, Dayton and I ran from the

A turkey finishing house in northeast Arkansas.
PHOTOGRAPH BY TANJA MCKAY.

truck to the facility. We began to collect our samples. Dayton went to the middle of the house, while I stayed near one end of the facility. Just as I turned my head to look down the house, a lightning bolt hit the roof. The sound was deafening as the electrical surge traveled through the building. Dayton immediately dropped down to his knees at the same time a thousand turkeys hit the ground. I froze and waited for the worst. The turkeys fell silent for a brief moment in time, but they quickly recovered and resumed their activity shortly after the boom. Fortunately, there were no casualties. No turkeys ended up on a pre-Thanksgiving platter and I still had all my fingers and toes. However, the lightning did cause havoc in the electrical wiring, and it was another week before electricity was restored to the facility.

Although working in the poultry facilities was a dusty and dirty job, traveling to these facilities was amazing. As we traveled the winding country roads of the Ozarks, we were able to see the changing flora of each season. Small buttercups popped their heads out of the soil in spring, while blue chicory painted blue streaks along the ditches in July. Queen Anne's lace swayed delicately in the breeze, while roadrunners and deer often crossed our path as we drove along endless dirt roads. The rolling hills shed their summer colors in autumn, becoming an artist's pallet of reds, orange, and yellow.

It was in western Arkansas where I was first introduced to a small fruit called the persimmon. One day in late September we stopped beside a dirt road and Dayton picked a small yellow-orange fruit from a nearby tree. He brought it back to the truck and insisted that I try what he described as a fresh succulent fruit. Being Canadian and not knowing too much about the flora of Arkansas, I proceeded to bite the still-firm flesh. I was quite taken by surprise when the unimaginable taste of the green persimmon hit my tongue and caused my lips to pucker. This unripe fruit was so astringent that I was saliva free for the rest of the trip home. A few weeks later, as we drove by the same tree, Dayton insisted on me trying this fruit again. This time the persimmons were red-orange and much softer in texture. I was a bit wary, but I decided to give it a second tasting. To my astonishment, it was soft and ripe with a sweet flavor. My first thought was that this would make a delightful preserve for my Thanksgiving feast. Persimmons have been on my Thanksgiving menu many times since then.

Lunch breaks on the road usually involved fast food. Since we were interested in flies and their association with disease transmission, we also collected flies around these restaurants. We would finish our meal, put on our white protective gear, and proceed to the trash cans that were usually situated in the back. One day a fellow graduate student accompanied us on our trip. He decided to take a short siesta on the lawn while we collected flies. That day the restaurant manager came out and asked us if we were part of some government agency, there to collect evidence from the crime scene. "What crime scene," we thought. What she interpreted as the body of some unknown crime victim mysteriously placed on their lawn overnight was fortunately our sleeping graduate student. He luckily awoke, allowing us to explain this unusual scene.

We usually visited the broiler-breeder houses early in the week to release parasitic wasps. Early one morning as we were traveling the dirt roads to one of the facilities, we encountered a family of wild turkeys. We stopped for a few minutes to watch them feed beside the road. Their plump bodies immediately stimulated visions of my Thanksgiving menu. Now they would add a fine, wild, new twist to my feast. However, my thoughts of adding them to my list were quickly erased as they scurried into the brush due to the sound of an approaching four-wheeler. I could not believe what I was seeing. To my amazement, flying toward us on the four-wheeler was a heavyset man with a very large package of approximately fifty rolls of toilet paper delicately balanced on the steering wheel in front of him. We were in the middle of nowhere and where this gentleman was headed remains a mystery. Sadly, my vision of a wild turkey feast was obliterated by toilet paper.

As we traveled on down the gravel road, I cleared my head and began thinking about the work we needed to do at the next facility. But my thoughts were suddenly interrupted when Dayton abruptly put on the brakes. Luckily, I was wearing my seat belt. He immediately put the vehicle in reverse, and we stopped in front of a dilapidated red mailbox. We looked at each other in astonishment and asked each other if we were seeing the same thing. A rusty old truck was parked in a driveway. Both doors were open and lying across the seat was a very well-endowed woman. We likely would not have stopped had she been fully clothed, but in this case, she was very much exposed and getting a well-defined Arkansas suntan. My boss and I looked at each other, shook our heads in amazement, and went on our way.

That November my Thanksgiving dinner was well planned. Although I did not serve wild turkey, the persimmons made a nice addition to the meal. As I sat down with family and friends to a full plate of turkey, mashed potatoes, and stuffing, I recalled these memorable events that occurred during my travels to the poultry facilities. Flashbacks of collecting flies and releasing wasps became intermingled with pleasant and unforgettable visions of the Ozarks.

Additional Readings

Godfray, H.C.J. 1994. *Parasitoids.* Princeton, NJ: Princeton University Press.

Greenburg, B. 1971. *Flies and disease.* Vol. 1: *Ecology, classification, and biotic associations.* Princeton, NJ: Princeton University Press.

McKay, T., and T. D. Galloway. 1999. Survey and release of parasitoids (Hymenoptera) attacking house and stable flies (Diptera: Muscidae) in dairy operations. *Canadian Entomologist* 131:743–756.

Rutz, D. A., and R. C. Axtell. 1981. House fly (*Musca domestica*) control in broiler-breeder poultry houses by pupal parasites (Hymenoptera: Pteromalidae): Indigenous parasite species and releases of *Muscidifurax raptor. Environmental Entomology* 18:51–55.

Szalanski, A. L., C. B. Owens, T. McKay, and C. D. Steelman. 2004. Detection of *Campylobacter* and *Escherichia coli* O157:H7 from filth flies by polymerase chain reaction. *Medical and Veterinary Entomology* 18:241–246.

Sir David Attenborough Visits Arkansas

STANLEY TRAUTH

❧ JOE, JOY, AND I had just arrived at the Best Western Inn in Hot Springs at about 2:35 PM on Sunday, July 30, 2006, and we were checking into the motel with some degree of difficulty. I told the desk clerk my room was being paid for by the Attenborough party. She appeared to be somewhat confused and frustrated for a moment, but then noted that a six-room block had been reserved under that name, and my name was included. Joe was also excited to hear that he had been assigned to one of the rooms.

Joe Milanovich, my graduate student, had just completed two years of intensive field research for his master's degree. He had studied the reproductive ecology of a unique population of the western slimy sala-mander, *Plethodon albagula*. The uniqueness here lies in the fact that females from this population annually migrate to an abandoned mine shaft (called Spillway Mine) to lay their eggs. This particular study site, near Blakely Mountain Dam and situated high above the shoreline of Lake Ouachita, had been under investigation by a U. S. Forest Service field biologist, David A. Saugey, for nearly twenty years; I began studying the mine site seven years ago.

You might ask what makes this salamander study site so special to researchers. It is simply because the nesting females are in large numbers and can be easily observed and photographed as they brood their eggs. The brooding period, during which one would never get a chance to find a nesting female in the wild, may last up to four months. Few salamander ecologists have ever witnessed such a rare event—a spectacle that occurs annually in Spillway Mine.

113

As Joe signed for his room, his exuberance could not be contained. "They actually reserved a room for me!" he said with a smile from ear to ear.

I told him that many times during the last six months I had given his name to Paul Williams and Nikki Stew, both members of the Attenborough reconnaissance and sync team. They also understood that Joe's knowledge about the life history of the slimy salamander at Spillway Mine would come in handy during the preparation of Sir David's audio script. Joe and I had actually met Nikki a month earlier during a pre-staging visit to the mine. She was in charge of laying out the exact details of the planned visit by the British Broadcasting Corporation (BBC). Still, Joe seemed delighted just to have his name included on the register.

Joy, my wife, had been easily persuaded to come along with Joe and me to Hot Springs. She kept reminding me that someone other than me was going to have to be the "official photographer" of all events. I wasn't too thrilled to have to give up my trusty camera, but that made good sense. As a high school science teacher for seventeen years and now a PhD candidate and instructor in the Department of Biological Sciences at Arkansas State University for four years, she was well aware of the significance of the next two days. She, in fact, owns some of Sir David Attenborough's previous nature documentaries, which she has used in her classes, and he was actually coming to film in Arkansas! She showed reserved excitement, but expressed ample anticipation for what was about to transpire. It was difficult for Joe and me to remain reserved.

For almost a year, I had awaited and eagerly anticipated the arrival of Sir David and the BBC. All of this excitement was brought about by a once-in-a-lifetime opportunity at a national meeting of herpetologists in Tampa, Florida (in July 2005) and now was actually culminating in the present course of events. While attending this meeting with a former PhD student of mine (Malcolm McCallum), I learned that Malcolm, on a whim, had responded via e-mail to an advertisement distributed at the meeting by the BBC. They were requesting information about any unusual behavior or research being conducted on amphibians and/or reptiles from anyone at this meeting. Malcolm explained to the BBC several aspects of my salamander research at the Blakely Mountain Dam study site and provided them with my e-mail address. I was pleasantly surprised when I received an e-mail message from Paul Williams three months later requesting more information about my research at Spillway Mine.

Could this event actually be happening? The legendary Sir David Attenborough, the most prolific natural history writer and documentarian of the twentieth century—a knighted citizen of the British crown and torchbearer of historic proportions for the BBC—was really coming to Arkansas to film an episode on salamanders for the last natural history segment of his illustrious career! Sir David was eighty years of age, and this forthcoming series, *Life in Cold Blood* (to be aired in 2008), would be the twenty-first and last of Sir David's fabulous documentaries on the natural world for the BBC. His first series of documentaries was *Zoo Quest*, which began in 1954 and ended in 1964. I can still visually recall segments from the thirteen-part series, *Life on Earth*, which appeared in 1979. He has also published sixteen books compiled from information presented in these documentaries.

It was even harder to imagine that the final five-part series was focusing on the world's amazing herpetofauna (covering all groups of amphibians and reptiles) and might include footage on salamander behavior recorded at a tiny mine shaft located in Arkansas. I held my breath with every communication with the BBC. Would they schedule time to actually come to my study site? Every preliminary step and every turn of events during the past nine months kept me saying to myself that this was really not going to happen. Something had to spoil this once-in-a-lifetime opportunity to meet and converse with Sir David Attenborough. And now, in fact, nearly a year's worth of planning, scheduling, and anticipation was about to be realized.

Joy and I stepped out of the foyer of the inn to grab some papers from our vehicle when we observed two Chevy Suburbans pull up behind us. As soon as I saw the large amount of gear in the back of one of the vehicles, I knew that the BBC and Sir David had arrived at our rendezvous point. Out of the first vehicle stepped the BBC filming crew including Scott Alexander (director), Kevin Flay (sync cameraman), and Andrew Yarme (sound recordist). I greeted them with enthusiasm but quickly looked toward the second vehicle. Ruth Flowers (personal assistant to Sir David) came up to greet me; she had been driving the second vehicle. And finally, behind all of them walked Sir David in casual attire. I approached Sir David, shook hands with him, and asked how his flights had been during the day. I was told that it had been a long day.

They had just arrived in Hot Springs from Dallas but had left early in the morning from Tucson, Arizona, where they had been filming lizard and snake behavior for about four days. Their departure time from Tucson was around 6:30 AM; therefore, all were up at 4:30 to get to the airport in plenty of time to check their many containers of filming gear.

I had been told that Sir David, although still a spry gentleman, had been slowed somewhat in recent years by a hip ailment. During the pre-staging visit with Nikki back in June, Joe and I were told that Sir David might not be able to transverse the inclined crawlspace down into the abandoned mineshaft, the site where most of the filming would take place. We had considered several alternative filming locations and options, including filming a segment at an easily accessible surrogate mineshaft located in the Caddo Mountains of southwestern Arkansas. At the last moment this option was dropped from the schedule.

The BBC crew and Sir David were ravenous after traveling all day (subsisting on peanuts and pretzels), so we decided to "lunch" at Chili's restaurant in late afternoon. Joy alertly grabbed her camera during the meal, and we had a waitress photograph all of us, except Ruth, who ducked out of the way to avoid the embarrassment of a bad hair day. Later that afternoon, Joe, Joy, and I took Scott, Kevin, and Andrew to survey the habitat surrounding the mine, and they basically rehearsed segments for the next day's filming activities. After returning to Hot Springs at about 7:30 PM, all of us cleaned up and then drove to the Outback restaurant for a late-evening meal.

We soon discovered that Sir David and the rest of the BBC team were quite personable and likeable. We bathed in this social atmosphere of

Lunch at Chili's restaurant. *Clockwise from left:* Joe Milanovich, Kevin Flay, Sir David Attenborough, Joy Trauth, Stanley Trauth, Scott Alexander, and Andrew Yarme.

British banter, storytelling, and camaraderie for several hours—a most extraordinary and incredible experience during a most amazing event. As Joe retired to his motel room that night, which was right next to Sir David's, he exclaimed, "I can't believe I'm rooming next to Sir David Attenborough!" I have no idea how many people Joe called on his cell phone to relay that day's happenings before getting to sleep.

The next morning things seemed to be different. Where had the joviality gone? We soon realized that the experienced BBC team was now ready to get down to the business at hand, and everyone, including Sir David, had become somewhat solemn and intense.

We arrived at the departure road leading to Spillway Mine at around 9:00 AM on Monday, July 31. Fortunately, I was able to pre-arrange logistical assistance with the U.S. Army Corps of Engineers (USACE). Several volunteers were ready to transport the gear (the seventeen or so containers of supplies and filming equipment) and us into the study area. Mr. Johnny Cantrell, district biologist for the USACE, led this team and provided us with two four-wheel-drive "mules." With the help of two young summer interns, everyone and everything was ferried back and forth from the mine to the vehicle parking area. Mr. Cantrell's presence was certainly fortuitous when USACE lawn-mowing operations began in the area near the mine and produced a loud noise distraction; he was able to quickly get the mowers and trimmers relocated to an area far from the filming. At the minor cost of several stings, he and his assistants also removed a yellow-jacket nest from beneath a downed log, which was lying across the pathway to the mine. Overall, their participation was an invaluable addition to the filming event and made Sir David's visit go off without a hitch.

Ruth, Sir David's trusted aide for around eighteen years, reminded us about several filming imperatives—things we, as observers, could do and could not do during filming. The most important rule was to not talk to Sir David just before filming a segment. It's at this time that he enters into an almost-hypnotic trance as he prepares to deliver those most-distinctive phrases in that most-recognizable and unmistakable voice. And certainly, no photography of him or the BBC crew was allowed immediately before or during filming. Some photography was allowed between takes. Joy took full advantage of those opportunities, which resulted in a remarkable set of photographs. Several of these are shown in the figures.

We all found Attenborough to be personable, very knowledgeable, and often funny. At one point Joy was standing beside him while the director read the script so the cameraman could lay out the scene. Sir David turned to her and said, "I'm not really going to say that," and he didn't.

Scott Alexander, Kevin Flay, and Stanley Trauth discuss the site for filming the first scene along the trail to Spillway Mine.

PHOTOGRAPH BY JOY TRAUTH.

Scott Alexander reads through the script with Sir David Attenborough before shooting the first scene.

PHOTOGRAPH BY JOY TRAUTH.

Kevin Flay and Andrew Yarme adjust the camera angle and sound equipment before shooting Sir David Attenborough entering Spillway Mine.

Joe Milanovich, Stanley Trauth, Sir David Attenborough, David Saugey, and Betty Crump between shoots. David Saugey and Betty Crump are U.S. Forest Service personnel.

We abided by all the BBC's conditions, although it was very difficult to explain this system to the newspaper teams from the *Hot Springs Sentinel* and the *Arkansas Democrat-Gazette*, who arrived, as per my request, later that afternoon. They wanted to photograph everything and everyone in and out of the mine.

Joe and I were inside Spillway Mine watching Sir David and the BBC team film take after take for nearly three hours. We stood apart from the filming episodes for most of this time. I would nudge Joe from time to time as we both stood in the dark mesmerized into disbelief by Sir David's delivery during each take. Sir David called me over to his chair during a brief respite between takes and asked me some scientific questions about the biology of the western slimy salamander. Then, unbelievably, he discarded the written script and used my comments almost verbatim in the next take. It was a humbling moment for me, and one that I will never forget.

I was finally asked to participate in one of the last filming sequences in which a salamander was to be placed on a rock perch along the mine's

Sir David Attenborough mentally prepares for the
next scene inside Spillway Mine.
PHOTOGRAPH BY STANLEY TRAUTH.

wall, and at the same time a close-up, infra-red camera was to be placed on one side of the salamander with Sir David's face inches away on the other side. All five of us (the filming crew, Sir David, and I) stood squeezed together into a space less than the size of a small closet. It took three takes of that segment to get it just right—Sir David looking at the salamander and talking, the salamander remaining motionless (with me holding it by the tail just seconds before filming), a camera rolling, and all lights turned off. What an extraordinary experience it was!

I became convinced that I had to have a photograph of Sir David in the mine, so I sent Joe out of the mine to get a digital camera. As Sir David paused between takes and was contemplating the next script, I photographed him during a reflective moment. Finally, I had the photograph I had desired from day one of this most-incredible adventure. As filming concluded late in the afternoon and all photo ops and interviews were finished, we walked (and rode) peacefully away from Spillway Mine with the knowledge that this was an irreplaceable moment, and nothing could quite match the magical time spent with Sir David Attenborough.

I write this piece at a point in time approximately two months following that ever-so-brief, twenty-four-hour period, a most extraordinary day in my life as a herpetologist and a field biologist. Although the BBC film crew will return to Spillway Mine to film the salamanders again later this year, nothing can replace the lasting memories seated in my mind during those two wonderful days in late July 2006 when Sir David Attenborough visited Arkansas.

Previous Nature Documentaries by Sir David Attenborough

1954–64 *Zoo Quest*
1975 *The Explorers*
1976 *The Tribal Eye*
1977 *Wildlife on One*
1979 *Life on Earth*
1984 *The Living Planet*
1987 *The First Eden*
1989 *Lost Worlds, Vanished Lives*
1990 *The Trials of Life*
1993 *Wildlife 10*
1993 *Life in the Freezer*
1995 *The Private Life of Plants*
1996 *Attenborough in Paradise*

1997 *The Wildlife Specials*
1998 *The Life of Birds*
2000 *State of the Planet*
2001 *The Blue Planet*
2002 *The Life of Mammals*
2005 *Life in the Undergrowth*
2006 *Planet Earth*
2008 *Life in Cold Blood*—in production

Cave Biology: It's Not a Job, It's an Adventure

ALDEMARO ROMERO

🐾 A GOOD PORTION OF MY scholarly work has dealt with cave fauna—cave fishes, to be more precise. In fact, cave fishes were the central theme of my doctoral dissertation in 1984, and to this day I continue to do work in that area. That is not to say that I am a scientist whose cave work has been an uneventful quest for data, nor am I an avid spelunker (cave explorer) who also happens to do science. Actually, many of my experiences in caves have been rather unusual, spanning many countries and dating back to the time before I was even a teenager. I will present my cave stories in chronological order as I moved from one country to another, from one circumstance to another.

Venezuela

When I was seven, my father bought a house in a suburban area on the fringes of the city where I was born: Caracas, Venezuela. Having always been a person interested in nature, I was delighted by the move. The fact that we had moved to a hilly area of the mountains that surround the capital of the country meant that I had the opportunity to wander around, explore new territories, and have childhood adventures in natural areas. In fact, my bedroom on the second story of my house faced one of those hills, so to me, walking and exploring was as easy as visiting a neighbor.

From my family's vantage point in the suburban hills, I was also able to witness some interesting political events from a unique viewpoint. Being able to overlook the city of Caracas from the surrounding hills meant that I could observe the planes flying all around during the coup d'état that in 1958 restored democracy in Venezuela. Those were turbulent years because shortly after that political shake-up, Fidel Castro took over the government in Cuba, and for some reason he put a great deal of effort into supporting the leftist guerrillas in Venezuela.

One day in 1961, when I was about ten years old, some of the new friends I had made in the neighborhood told me about a cave known as *La Cueva del Zamuro* (the Vulture's Cave) in one of the hills nearby. They asked me if I would like to walk there with them and I did not think twice. The cave lay at the heart of a large, pyramidal hill facing Caracas and was about a forty-five-minute walk from my home.

My friends and I strolled toward the cave while chattering like any other group of kids involved in a similar activity. As soon as we arrived at the cave, we could see it was not a natural cave. It looked more like an abandoned mine in which you could barely walk standing up without bumping your head against the ceiling. We were all carrying flashlights.

We had not walked more than ten feet into the cavern when we observed a couple of large bags. We opened them and saw that they were full of food, lots of canned food. We had just begun to sort out the cans while asking ourselves why someone would leave so much food in a remote area when someone with a deep voice and from well inside the cave yelled, "What do you want?"

Needless to say, we all ran out of the cave for miles without even looking back. As soon as we all got home, we told the story to our parents and some of them alerted the police. Two days later we learned through the TV news that the cave was being used by a guerilla group and that a group of "courageous kids" had discovered some kind of hideout for "subversives." So much for my first visit to the underground, geological or otherwise. Another less than pleasant experience in caves happened to me when I was just trying to visit one.

In 1979 my wife, Ana (also a biologist), and I had been hired to our first faculty positions at a new university in Venezuela. In fact, the university was so new that it had no students, so we had plenty of time on our hands.

The university was located in Coro, a state capital in western Venezuela. The town was between the sea and a mountainous region. That part of the country is known for being very, very hot, with regional temperature records well above 110 degrees F.

One day we heard about a rather cool area in the nearby mountains where there was a yet unexplored cave. My wife and I were intrigued, of course, and decided to visit the place. We were given detailed driving instructions and headed there at mid-morning. Once we arrived at the location, we realized that the trail to the cave went through a pasture where there were some cattle. We started walking and not even a minute had passed before my wife and I realized that each of us was covered with ticks—literally hundreds if not thousands of small, black ticks!

The ticks were everywhere, on our skin, scalps, clothing, underneath our fingernails. We rushed back toward our jeep and headed home, where we disposed of our clothing, got into swimsuits, and headed to the beach armed with eyebrow tweezers. Once we got to the beach, we sat at neck level in the water trying to kill by asphyxiation as many ticks as possible, while removing the rest from each other's faces and scalps and from under our fingernails using the tweezers. We looked like monkeys deparasitizing each other. It took us about two hours to get rid of every single little, black creature from our bodies.

We never tried to visit that cave again.

Coral Gables, Florida

After these failed attempts to visit caves early in my life, the next opportunity came, of all places, in Miami—where there are no caves.

My scientific career as a biospeleologist began at the University of Miami, Florida. My original intention was to study marine biology for my PhD, and the University of Miami had one of the best marine schools in the United States. So I went there and registered first to study English since at that time my proficiency in that language was little better than the ability to do some technical reading.

However, shortly after I arrived there, I was told that the marine school had many problems and that I would be better off if I stayed on the main campus and found a potential adviser in any area of interest for me. Since I was interested in both fish and behavior, I visited the office of Dr. Brian Partridge. Brian was a recently hired assistant professor who had worked on fish behavior at Oxford University, and one of the most interesting results of his experiments was that after artificially blinding some fish, he had shown that they were still capable of swimming and forming schools. That was interesting to me because at that time it was not clear how much vision and how much pressure sensing through their lateral line (a sensory system on the sides of most fishes, capable of detecting changes in pressure) was necessary to form schools. His experiments had shown that, at least in some cases, eyes were not necessary.

He was just turning his attention toward blind cave fishes when I visited him. I was just a candidate for graduate school speaking broken English. He was courteous but not particularly enthusiastic about my visit. I told him that I was at the university studying English and planned to enter graduate school in biology, and that in the meantime I wanted to keep my hands "wet" by doing some science. He wrote on a piece of paper the scientific name of a blind cave fish he intended to study, *Anoptichthys jordani,* and told me that if I wanted, I could come back on Monday and help him. That was on a Friday.

The existence of blind cave fishes was news to me, but I felt fascinated about those creatures. So I spent Saturday and Sunday at the library at the University of Miami trying to find everything that had been published about that species: I scanned all the volumes of the *Biological Abstracts,* a collection of references to most of the papers in biology since 1927. In those two days I was able to generate on note cards more than a hundred references of published papers about that species, and by reading the abstracts I learned that the species name that he had given me was probably incorrect and that most likely his intended study organism was a blind cave form of a surface fish known as the Mexican tetra, *Astyanax fasciatus.*

On Monday I showed up at Brian's office with a full set of note cards. As soon as I showed them to him, he was really impressed; and as I was telling him what I had learned (including about the correct name), his eyes kept widening larger and larger. He noticed my enthusiasm for the subject and he was caught up with it as well. He quickly showed me his lab, talked to me about his ideas . . . and offered to become my graduate adviser. I did not think twice, and a few months later I was a graduate student at the University of Miami and would dedicate many future years to the study of cave biology.

Costa Rica

My plan once I became a graduate student was to finish my coursework as quickly as possible so I could dedicate all of my time to studying blind cave fishes. I still remember that once I was admitted to the graduate school, Brian asked me what question I wanted to answer for my dissertation. My answer surprised him: I wanted to know how these fishes became blind and depigmented? The surprise was two-fold: I was proposing a rather BIG question that could have required years if not decades of work; the other reason was that this was not a typical answer to the question, "What is your hypothesis?" How I was going to answer it, I had no idea, nor did he, but that did not mean that I was afraid of tackling the problem.

In the meantime I had decided to take as many courses as possible, and I saw an opportunity that summer: a two-month course on tropical ecology organized by the Organization for Tropical Studies in Costa Rica. At the end I would receive eight graduate credits. Thus, the combination of credits and the incredible experience that I would gain spending two months doing field work made this a very tempting opportunity. In addition, I knew that the surface form of the fish *Astyanax fasciatus* is also found in Costa Rica, which meant that I would have the chance to see this species in its natural environment, although no blind cave fishes had been reported at that time for that Central American country.

In this course all students participated in group projects at many different field stations, and one of those stations was Palo Verde in a semi-dry forest in western Costa Rica. It happened that on the second day at that station as I was walking around looking for bodies of water where I might find "my" fish, I encountered a spring, and in the small pond next to it, there it was: my fish. Could it be that this tetra (as it is known in the aquarium fish trade) was entering a subterranean source of water and, if so, could this be a living example of cave colonization?

Given the short time of the course and our stay at that station, I had no time to conduct serious research; but as soon as I got back to Miami, I wrote a grant proposal in order to return to Costa Rica and do some field work in that area. After securing the funding, I went back with a portable video-recording system in order to record any possible behavior of the fish entering and exiting this subterranean source of water. At that time "portable video" meant a rather large black-and-white camera with a separate, bulky video recorder, using Betamax tapes.

The pond was surrounded by forest, and in my first day as I was setting up the camera, I heard a troop of howler monkeys (*Alouatta palliata*) roaming through the canopy of the forest. As they got closer and closer to me, they became noisier and noisier. Since I had work to do, I did not pay much attention to them. But they became really agitated and started to throw branches of trees at me. I realized that I was probably in their drinking pond and they wanted me to go away, but I figured that if I ignored them, they would go away. So I continued to do my work, although I became concerned that if they kept throwing branches at me, some of those branches would fall onto the water and would disturb the fish whose behavior I was trying to record. When I was finally focusing my

camera, I started feeling a warm fluid on my back: the monkeys were peeing on me!

Since no monkey was going to deter me from doing my observations,
I set up all my equipment in a tent (a dangerous proposition when you are
working with electronic equipment in the middle of the summer in tropical Costa Rica). Well, I was able to record the behavior; the monkeys
relented and probably moved on to another pond, and I could videotape
the fish entering and exiting the spring. (I would later discover that they
used the cave as a refuge from predators, mostly fishing bats.)

Aldemaro Romero filming blind cave fish
at a spring in Palo Verde, Costa Rica.
PHOTOGRAPH BY ANA ROMERO.

Once I had the data and tapes that I worked so hard for several weeks to obtain, it was time to return to San José, the capital of Costa Rica. I went to the nearest port by horse to be transported with my equipment to the other side of the river. The boatman approached me and I passed on to him all the paraphernalia I was carrying. Then I boarded the boat and went to the other side of the river. We both disembarked at the same time once we arrived at the other shore. The problem was that the boatman had not anchored the boat to any pole, so as soon as our feet were on shore, the boat started to drift downstream. "The boat!" I screamed, and at that point the boatman replied, "I do not know how to swim." Well, there it was, a boat carrying all my possessions going down the river, probably heading to the ocean with all the tapes and data in it. I did not think twice and jumped into the water, swimming as fast as I could. I clung to the boat and pushed it toward the shore. Once there, I made sure that the rope was tied to a tree, and then the boatman caught up with me. Soaking wet, I went to get the jeep I had rented, drove to where the boat was, and put all the equipment and tapes in the jeep.

It had been quite an adventure. But weeks of work had not been lost. My work in Costa Rica resulted in a couple of papers and became an important part of my doctoral dissertation. But, I had had no real cave experiences yet.

Mexico

To really study the cave fish, I had to go to Mexico to the caves in La Sierra del Abra in the San Luis de Potosí region, where nearly thirty cave fish populations of the Mexican cave tetra had been found. The caves had been well mapped by Robert Mitchell and his colleagues in the 1970s. So the question was not so much whether we could find the caves, but whether we could get the collecting permits to be able to explore them, find and collect the fish, and study them for as long as needed. One thing I was interested in seeing was how they responded to light. Yes, it sounds strange to study the responses to light among fishes that are blind, but it happens that the American ichthyologist Charles Breder had noticed in the 1940s that some of the individuals he had collected in Mexico did respond to light, probably through their pineal gland, a hormone-producing, light-sensitive organ located near the brain. So the issue was an intriguing one to me.

I first made an exploratory trip to Mexico in order to deal with the paperwork for the collecting permit, meet a local caver who could accompany me in my explorations (it is never a good idea to adventure alone into caves), and get a "feeling" for the area. For example, what kind of transportation was needed to get to the caves? What kind of gear did I need? Could I find a good hotel for me and my family where I could conduct some of the experiments with the fish? Once I had answered all those questions, I got my rabies shots (many of the caves are inhabited by bats), got my gear (some of the caves were vertical ones up to 240 feet deep), and then headed down to Mexico.

Once I got to the study area, I settled with my family in a cabin at a local hotel and then got ready for my first cave exploration. The first caves I visited had easy access: horizontal and wide enough. Then came the vertical ones and they were really challenging: to descend and (especially) ascend vertically for about 240 feet carrying a lot of gear—including old-fashion video cameras, recorders, and buckets with fish—is not fun. But everything went well.

Then the local caver I had hired to accompany me on my visits to the caves had to leave, but I still had a few caves to visit. Fortunately, they were all horizontal ones, so they did not look particularly risky. In any case, every morning before leaving for the cave, I told my wife where I was going and at what time I should be expected back. In an era with no cell phones and in the middle of nowhere in Mexico, that was the best I could do.

I found one of the caves. As I always am, I was very careful making sure that all of my gear was in order, with the headlamp and flashlights working properly, as well as all of the videotape equipment. I started to walk into the cave, but from the beginning I got the sense that something was wrong. I could not see as well as usual. I tried to adjust the headlamp but yet things did not seem right. Then I realized that I had made a very stupid mistake. I had walked into the cave still wearing my sunglasses! So much for careful preparation. Well, I then took the sunglasses off and at that very moment I heard something strange. I looked down, and there just three feet away from me were several small rattlesnakes, which started to rattle intensely as soon as I pointed the light from the headlamp toward them. Despite the fact that I always wear boots when doing field work, I am sure it would not have been a nice experience to step on half a dozen or so rattlesnakes.

After exploring the cave and avoiding any direct contact with the snakes on my way out, I stopped by a nearby *caserío* or small town. I mentioned what had happened to me with the snakes while drinking a soda in the only local establishment that sold food. The locals told me that those snakes had been "placed" there by the gods to protect an alleged

Aztec treasure. In the beginning I was amused by the story, but then they started to ask me more and more questions and I realized that they took me for a treasure hunter.

As the questioning became more and more aggressive, I decided to leave, but I was surrounded by a crowd, which kept looking at my bags while asking all kinds of questions. Then I remembered that I was carrying with me some live fish, and I showed them to the locals, who were quite intrigued by the jars of fish. Then I started to speak like a real nerd, using all kinds of scientific jargon. I said things such as "I am studying the photoresponses of *Astyanax fasciatus* in order to see how scotophilia works as a behavioral response from their pineal organ" and other things along those lines. People started looking at me as if I needed a straight jacket. At that very moment I got my stuff in the car and left.

Other experiences were also frightening, although for different reasons. Another horizontal cave I visited was in a mining area. The cave looked easy enough, but as I walked into it, the passages became narrower and narrower to the point that I had to crawl to get to the hall where the pond with the blind fish was. While I was crawling along thirty feet of passages, I started to think what would happen if at that very moment an earthquake occurred. As though having brought the earthquake with my mind, the earth started to shake with a deep, low-frequency sound. I thought that was my end. I stopped crawling and waited for the worst, but having previously lived through a couple of earthquakes, I thought this one seemed different. The shaking was very regular with a combination of noises that were almost rhythmic. But, of course, I had never before been underground while an earthquake was taking place. Then I realized that there was no such earthquake: all the noise and trembling of the ground was a cargo train, just passing above me.

Once it was time to go back to Miami, I put my live fish in a bucket and prepared all the permits that were required in order to carry my fish on the plane. In order to keep the fish alive, I was carrying with me a portable air pump, which I used while I was at the airport, and a few "oxygen pills," the type of effervescent pills that you put in the water that can provide oxygen to the fish for a few hours. These pills were small and black.

When I arrived at the Miami International Airport and was asked at customs if I had anything to declare, I said "yes," explained about the fish, and was directed to the agriculture inspector. As soon as I had placed the bucket with the fish on his counter, I showed him the paperwork. He looked at it like he was not really sure what he was supposed to look for and then he looked into the bucket with curiosity. After glancing at it for about twenty seconds, he asked me, "Do you have a permit for the snails too?" I looked at him and asked, "What snails?" He replied, "Those at the bottom of the bucket." Thinking that the water might have been contaminated with snails, I looked into the bucket and then realized that the agriculture inspector thought that the black oxygen pills were snails. I laughed. However one wonders about the effectiveness of government officials who cannot distinguish between a pill and a snail.

Trinidad

Trinidad is an island country northeast of Venezuela. Its fauna and flora are more related to those in South America than those of the other large island of that country, Tobago. Trinidad has a cave, the Cumaca Cave, known for having a blind cave catfish; and while I was still a graduate student, I decided to visit it in order to know more about it. After all, since the time this catfish had been discovered, there had been very little published information about it.

In 1983 I contacted the Selma Biological Station, a field laboratory where I could stay and from where I could go to explore the cave in question. I had made arrangements to be picked up by a local driver, who was to take me to the cave, but that morning beginning at about 4:00 AM, I woke up with a discomfort in my belly. In the beginning I did not think too much about it. I went to the restroom and back to my bed, but the pain became more and more acute. Because of the location of the pain, I started to think that I had appendicitis; however, I had no fever and when I lifted my leg while pressing the area of pain, I felt no difference. "It must be something else," I said to myself. So I woke up the field station manager, who took me to a local doctor who as soon as he saw me said, "You have a kidney stone." And his diagnosis was right on the mark. I had to leave the country but returned years later to study the blind catfish there.

In the year 2000 I returned with a student of mine, Joel Creswell, in order to observe the fish. By now I was more intrigued than ever. Based on what I had read, this blind cave catfish had been elusive at best. Since first described by the British ichthyologist John Richardson Norman in 1926 as a new genus and species, *Caecorhamdia urichi*, the fish had been seen by very few people. In fact, some of the few who had tried to collect it since then claimed that the fish could not be found.

When I finally visited the cave, I felt frustrated. This cavern is famous for hosting a colony of noisy oil birds (*Steatornis caripensis*) as well as a colony of bats and some other cave creatures. The cave is not particularly

Aldemaro Romero (*right*) with guide in Cumaca Cave in Trinidad.
PHOTOGRAPH BY JOEL CRESSWELL.

long (about three hundred feet) and is horizontal. The water is not deep, and although two divers died trying to explore the origin of its water at a pool at the end of the cave, it is actually a very safe and easy cave to explore. After spending one hour looking for the fish, I and my companions had not found even one. Was it possible that the fish in question had become extinct? After all, it had only been reported from that cave.

Tired of looking, I had almost decided to leave when I suddenly saw a quick reflection in the water. I asked my companions to turn off their flashlights while I turned on a portable video camera with infrared capabilities. Once I did so, I started to scan the waters with the camera, and then, surprise: dozens of fish started to appear from underneath the rocks, while reflecting the infrared source of light from their tapetum lucidum, a layer of tissue in their eyes that quite easily reflects low-intensity light ("cat's eyes").

But wasn't this catfish supposed to be blind and depigmented? After collecting a few specimens and studying all specimens of this species available from around the world, I came up with the conclusion that the blind cave catfish was just a form of the catfish *Rhamdia quelen*, quite common in that part of the world. The blind form was the product of isolation when the waters of the cave were disconnected from the nearby rivulet at the end of the nineteenth century and beginning of the twentieth. But beginning in the 1930s, rain precipitation had increased considerably in that part of the world, allowing the normal catfish to reinvade the cave and ecologically replace its blind derivative.

The fish was only observable by using infrared cameras because it was scotophilic, that is, stayed away from the light. That is why so many researchers in the past could not find the fish: they were using flashlights and the fish hid underneath the rocks in the cave stream in the presence of light. Somehow by turning off the flashlights, I saw the light, and one mystery, among the many concerning cave creatures, was solved.

Additional Readings

Romero, A. 1984. Behavior in an intermediate population of the subterranean-dwelling characid *Astyanax fasciatus*. *Environmental Biology of Fishes* 10:203–207.

———. 1984. Charles Marcus Breder, Jr., 1897–1983. *National Speleological Society News* 42:207–271.

———. 1985. Cave colonization by fish: Role of bat predation. *American Midland Naturalist* 113:7–12.

Romero, A., and J. Creswell. 2000. In search of the elusive "eyeless" cave fish of Trinidad, W.I. *National Speleological Society News* 58:282–283.

Romero, A., A. Singh, A. McKie, M. Manna, R. Baker, K. M. Paulson, and J. E. Creswell. 2002. Replacement of the Troglomorphic population of *Rhamdia quelen* (Pisces: Pimelodidae) by an Epigean population of the same species in the Cumaca Cave, Trinidad, West Indies. *Copeia* 2002:938–942.

Just Floatin' around Carriacou

RICHARD GRIPPO

🦎 SOMETHING BIG GRABBED my scuba tank. I was watching the tank spiral down into the depths in the fading, rippling glow of dusk, that half-light that seems to last forever in the tropics. I was surprised by how long the tank stayed in view as it sank. I had never dropped a tank in the twilight before, so I guessed it was the white epoxy paint on the aluminum tank that made it visible for so long. Suddenly, only the ends of the tank were showing. Something was blocking the middle of the tank from view. It was just at the limit of visibility, so it was hard for me to tell for sure, but I thought I saw the flash of a large tail about ten feet off to the side of the tank. The tank seemed to move back and forth in a slow shaking motion. Then, everything disappeared into the depths. What was down there?! We had been drifting for a while now and were probably over deep water where the big fish are.

What was I doing floating around in a tropical sea at dusk in waters known to contain sharks? Sharks, as every marine ecologist knows, are crepuscular and tend to feed mostly at dawn and dusk when the diurnal fish are just starting to lose their vision in the falling light and the nocturnal fish are still waking up and adjusting their sleepy eyes to the same light. My eyes were not sleepy. They were wide open with fright.

As an undergraduate student majoring in marine biology at Fairleigh Dickinson University (FDU) in New Jersey, I had looked forward to my senior semester in the U.S. Virgin Islands. I had been a commuter student my entire time at college, and this was my first chance to truly enjoy the "college experience." FDU had developed the West Indies Laboratory (WIL), a marine science teaching and research facility, on the eastern end of St. Croix. WIL came into existence through the generosity of the university's namesake, Fairleigh Dickinson Jr., who had extensive real-estate holdings on the island. He would occasionally show up at the lab and sometimes even good-naturedly wear a T-shirt given to him by FDU students with the popular saying "Fairly Ridiculous University" silk-screened on it. Being new to the dorm scene, I was not prepared for the question posed to me by Andy Romano, a friendly Brooklynite who loved the Yankees.

"Where ya' goin' for spring break?" he asked.

I had not thought about it at all. As a commuter student, all spring break had meant to me in the past was more time available to work as a bartender and cook, jobs I had taken to help put myself through college. After thinking about it for a second, I said, "I'm not going anywhere. I'm staying right here at the lab." I had quickly developed visions of the hordes of college students coming to St. Croix for *their* spring break. I figured that I would be able to pass as a local, especially with my carefully cultivated, three-month, deep tan; and I might even get lucky with some of the lovely young ladies, sure to arrive looking for a good time.

"Ya' can't stay at the lab. All the students get kicked outta da dorms, so the professes' and staff can getta break too. I'm flying home. I'm stoppin' in Florida on da way ta see da Yaankees in spring training. I get ta see Bucky Dent!" Bucky Dent was an all-star second baseman recently acquired by the Yankees through a trade.

I pondered this for a while. Flying back home to New Jersey was out of the question for me. Why go back to the place everyone was leaving and leave the place to which everyone was going? Anyway, it was too expensive to fly. I could try to stay in a hotel on St. Croix, but because the main source of income on this resort island is well-heeled tourists, there are no cheap places to stay—at least not in areas where I would feel safe staying. So, what to do?

Over the next few days I talked to other students about what they were going to do over spring break. To my amazement, most were going home to the East Coast. We had all gotten a little homesick, but I must have been one of those least bitten by that particular bug. I had spent almost twenty-two years living at home and was finding my independence to be intoxicating. I wanted an adventure! I wanted to see new places and try new things.

I decided to try to travel around the Caribbean a bit. Hmmm. How far could one get (and get back) in twelve days? Where could I stay that was cheap? My total budget was about $150 dollars. Even in the mid 1970s,

$15 per day was not going to purchase me much in the way of dining, overnight accommodations, and transportation. Somehow I would have to find someone else to pay for most of my adventure.

My solution came after talking to Hank the Dive Master. He told me that people were sometimes willing to pay, or at least give free passage, if you helped them sail their boats in the open waters between islands within the Caribbean basin. He called these people "shallow-water sailors" and figured that they were nervous about sailing alone in deep water. Actually, most of them were fine sailors—wealthy doctors, lawyers, and other professionals with sea-worthy boats—who were just a little apprehensive about going it alone over open water, out of sight of any land. Many weekend boat warriors get anxious when the flying fish start to appear, which generally indicates open ocean. Free passage was a small price for them to pay to have an extra deckhand to help with the sails, the docking of the boat, setting the anchor, and even fighting off the pirates that occasionally ply the waters of the sunny Caribbean. Concern with pirates may seem strange to those unfamiliar with the maritime Caribbean, but that area of the world has a rich tradition of piracy. After all, the island of Dead Chest, of the infamous pirate ditty, "Fifteen men and a Dead Man's Chest . . . yo ho ho and a bottle of rum," about the fate of Blackbeard's mutinous crew, is located in the British Virgin Islands in the northern portion of the basin.

Whatever the reasons for offering free passage, it was up to me to find the erstwhile captains who wanted to provide it. And where does one find yachts big enough to require a temporary extra crew member? Why, the yacht club, of course. The east end of St. Croix has had a yacht club for many years. The club dock is situated next to the West Indies Laboratory's dock. I had done a little work for some members of the club, mainly scraping algae off the bottom of a few of their boats using snorkeling gear, so the manager of the club knew me a bit and had an idea about my sailing experience. I was by no means an accomplished sailor, but I knew the difference between a jenny and a spinnaker; I understood what it was like to be "beating to the wind," and I knew how to reef the mainsail. Most importantly, I had a strong back for winching the jib back and forth as the boat tacked. I told him that I was interested in crewing for anyone sailing east toward St. Martin, the logical first leg of my journey. He looked at me interestedly, like he had just found the solution to a problem that had been bothering him for a while.

"I know of someone who has been talking about heading toward the French West Indies but seems to keep postponing his departure. I think he is a little nervous about going blue water with only his wife to crew. Last I heard he was thinking about leaving early next week. He can probably put off the trip a few more days until your spring break starts," he said.

Wow! Five minutes of "work" and I had my first leg booked! This was going to be easy, I thought. Of course, beginners luck usually only happens in the beginning. I still had to convince my teacher to give me the final exam early for the current course (each course was taught successively at WIL), so I would have as much time as possible to travel.

Six days later I was swinging my daypack and game bag with snorkel gear aboard the *Serendipity* at the break of dawn. It was a thirty-nine-foot Irwin, a beautiful boat with a galley and even a tiny stateroom. When I met the captain, a retired physician from Miami who loved the Caribbean, he seemed a bit hesitant about taking me on for the passage. Perhaps he was a bit embarrassed that he needed help sailing his boat. The deal maker came when I mentioned in passing that I had been working my way through college as a bartender and chef-in-training under a French cook from Montreal.

"Oh!" his wife said excitedly, "Can you make chicken cordon bleu?" This was a very popular dish in the 1970s, especially for those who thought themselves sophisticated diners who appreciated fine French cuisine. It is really just chicken, pounded, browned, and rolled up with ham and Swiss cheese inside, then baked. It is not much harder to make than a grilled cheese sandwich. The addition of a simple parmesan-cheese-based Mornay sauce made it into a gourmet dish for most people, I guess. When I assured the misses that chicken cordon blue would be no problem, even on their gimballed stove, she was insistent that I come and cook the dish during the passage.

The twelve-hour trip across about seventy miles of open ocean from St. Croix to St. Martin was a bit windy but otherwise quite uneventful. The captain knew what he was doing, his wife was experienced, and with modern navigation aids, charting our course was not a problem. We were beating into the wind most of the way, working against the easterlies so prevalent in that part of the world, but the ship was seaworthy and took the rolling swells in stride. I cranked the winches some and helped trim the boat, but my presence was not critical. Really, I was along mostly in the event of bad weather, which never materialized.

I finally made myself useful by preparing the chicken dish on the gimballed range, designed to stay horizontal as the boat tilts. It is a bit of a challenge to cook below deck with your meal always in imminent danger of sliding off the stove or out of the oven and onto your lap. Thankfully, the *Serendipity* had pot clamps to hold the cookware in place and a galley strap to hold me in place while I cooked. Served with wild rice and buttered peas, the meal was a hit. Sitting in the cockpit afterwards under the blue sky with glasses of Chablis, we started talking about the pros and cons of my planned final destination, St. Kitts, and its smaller sister island, Nevis. Hank the Dive Master had said they were the most beautiful islands in the Caribbean, with lush tropical forests not unlike what one would see in the South Pacific. I was looking forward to hanging out on the beaches and carousing with fellow spring breakers.

"Those are not really islands for spring break," the doctor said, disturbing my reverie. "They are more for the golf resort/country club set. Both islands were originally very wealthy from productive sugar cane plantations. There is still a lot of old money on the islands. There *is* still a lot of natural beauty, but the reefs around those islands have not done so well with the development caused by tourism. If I wanted to go to an island that is truly off the beaten path, I would go to Carriacou."

"Carriacou? Where's that?" I had never heard of the place.

"It is a small island near Grenada. It has great reefs, fantastic snorkeling and diving."

I had no clue where Grenada was either, but I vaguely recalled some of the students saying something about a medical school starting up there.

"Carriacou is off the beaten track right now, but when the medical school on Grenada gets going there will probably be a lot of people going there and it won't be the same," he said, confirming what little I already knew about the island.

Nothing more was said about Carriacou, but I was now feeling a bit dissatisfied with my plans. If Nevis and St. Kitts were really only for "old people," then where would I go instead? The answer came to me soon after we hit port on St. Martin. We docked in a harbor called Oyster Pond, located on the eastern side of St. Martin. Coming in, we had following waves that made finding and staying in the harbor channel a hair-raising experience; as I clung to a handrail, I wondered more than once why they picked this area for a harbor, considering it was directly exposed to the southern Atlantic and the waves seemed to have been building all the way from Africa. However, once inside the harbor, the water was extremely calm; and I realized that its popularity was probably because one could prepare and eat dinner here with complete ease, unlike my meal prepared below deck while underway.

After docking the boat, the doctor quickly disappeared into the Customs building to get through the paperwork. I was hesitant about doing the same thing because I had no passport, which would supposedly make my "check-in" onto the island a long, drawn-out process, even though, in the end, I was sure to be allowed to stay and spend my tourist dollars (of which I had very few, but St. Martin did not know that!). Plus, I would then have to face the reality of trying to find another boat, one that was headed to Nevis or St. Kitts. Before I could drag myself up to the Customs building, the doctor emerged and excitedly came down onto the floating dock to which we were moored.

"Guess what?!" he said, arching his eyebrows enthusiastically. "I have found you a boat ride to Grenada! One of my colleagues from Florida is thinking about teaching at St. Georges [the then-new medical school on Grenada]. He is heading there in his Marlow to check it out and would not mind having you along to spell him at the tiller. He could take you all the way to Grenada or drop you off on Carriacou!"

Whoa! All of a sudden I would be changing from going about fifty miles further down-island to going about five hundred miles! That was an awfully long way to sail a boat. Surely, I did not have enough time to get there and back. I told this to the doctor.

"It's not a sailboat; it's a motor yacht. He wants to cruise directly to Grenada, meet with the medical school people about a teaching position, and then slowly work his way back. He would not mind having you along to spell him at the wheel. He could get you there in about two days. His boat can cruise at twenty knots easy! He has a big boat," he added wistfully. I got the impression that a big motor yacht was something that had been on the doctor's mind for a while. "Oh, and I mentioned you could cook. His wife liked that. Better be prepared to whip up something good!"

And that was how I came to go to the island of Carriacou. It is located about twenty miles north of Grenada in the Grenadine Island chain, part of the Windward Islands, West Indies. Carriacou is part of the tri-island nation of Grenada, Carriacou, and Petit Martinique; and though small, it is still the largest Grenadine Island. Carriacou was at one time intensely farmed for cotton, but the soil was depleted and much of it has eroded away. The economy is slowly converting from agriculture to tourism, but like so many small Caribbean islands (and some countries, like Belize), the lack of a deepwater port has hampered development.

The trip from St. Martin to Carriacou was fun. The boat I was on was not really a luxury yacht but more like a work boat that had made some concessions to comfort. It was rather narrow in relation to its length, which made it rather crowded below, but it had no problems slicing through the waves even in following seas. The skipper acted like he was in a race with everybody, and as soon as he spotted a ship on the horizon, the chase was on until we caught and passed it. We virtually flew by the many islands of the West Indies. St. Kitts and Nevis were as beautiful as Hank the Dive Master had said. Guadeloupe was a huge island where we stopped briefly to pick up some supplies, including those needed for my now infamous French cooking. And, for the second time in three days, I made chicken cordon bleu with Mornay sauce. The taste was a bit different because I had to use goat cheese for both the chicken and the sauce, but it gave the dish a distinct Caribbean accent that I am sure even true French cooks would have approved.

We passed Dominique and then Martinique in the dark. St. Lucia was next; our nocturnal cruise-by was made more memorable by bonfires and fireworks on the beach. We finally took a break in a sheltered bay on St. Vincent. For the first time on my trip, I slept below deck, isolated from the sea breeze but enjoying the comfort of air conditioning.

We got underway at daybreak. The boat passed a series of small undeveloped islands one after another. After about two hours of this, yet another small island came into view. This was a bit larger than the rest and was fairly developed. Finally, Carriacou! The doctor had a medical-school friend who had a vacation home there (there seemed to be a community of sea-faring physicians in the Caribbean who all knew each other and helped each other out, as well as quietly but persistently played a game of one-upmanship with regard to boats) and would put me up for a night until I found a cheap place to stay. As it turned out, I was able to extend my free-loading visit by yet again preparing a meal of poultry and udder discharge. "When I get back from this trip I am not going to make this dish for a *long* time," I thought to myself as I pounded out the chicken breasts. At least the kitchen I was in was not pitching and yawing and trying to throw hot oil onto me, and from the kitchen window I could see beautiful African tulip, bougainvillea, poinsettia, and heliconia plants. But I still had to use goat cheese.

As it turned out, there were quite a few American spring breakers even on this tiny island. There were also students from other countries, especially Europe and Australia. It seemed that many people had heard about this "best kept secret of the Caribbean." A number of visitors were divers and had brought snorkeling gear, as I had. We snorkeled several great spots from the shore and collected fresh seafood to cook with driftwood and eat on the beach. Island rum was cheap (seventy-nine cents a quart), the ladies were friendly, and life was good.

One of the students said that he had visited a dive shop and they were talking about a dive at a place called Sister Rocks. It would be a fantastic dive for the next day or two because the tide would be running right by the reef at dusk, allowing for a fantastic dusk dive during which the divers could watch the changeover from diurnal to nocturnal fish. It required scuba tanks, but the dive would last over an hour because not much swimming effort was necessary. We could just descend at one end of the two-mile-long fringing reef and let the tidal current "fly" us past the reef. With tanks and a dive boat it would be expensive, but up until this point on my break I had spent very little money and could afford one scuba dive. The dive boat would be cheap if we could get a group of people to go and split the cost.

It turned out to be easy to convince a half-a-dozen people to partici-pate in such a unique opportunity, and we set up the dive. We decided to go to the end of the reef about forty-five minutes before sunset, descend down about twenty meters, adjust our buoyancy compensators to neutral buoyancy, and drift with the current. The dive boat would drift with the current above us and pick us up at the end of the reef before we drifted out to sea. At least, that was the plan. . . .

All went as planned, in the beginning. The view of the reef was fan-tastic with blue and brown chromis, parrotfish, angel fish, and damsel fish slowly sinking down closer and closer toward the reef while reef croakers, copper sweepers, squirrel fish, and other nocturnal marine animals were beginning to emerge from the reef crevices. The dive went by much more quickly then we had anticipated due to the effect of the four-knot current, and before we knew it, we had reached the end of the reef and were start-ing to head offshore. It was time to surface and get back in the dive boat. Heck, maybe there was time for another dive along at least part of the reef. However, when we got to the surface . . . nothing! Where was the dive boat? Bobbing in the waves and craning our necks, we could just pick out the boat at the other end of the reef. There appeared to be no one in the boat! Had the dive tender fallen overboard? Just then one of the Australian students started to yell at the boat. We all chimed in, seeing our predicament more as fun than as a real problem. Luckily, the breeze was blowing in the direction of the boat, and the tender's head popped up almost immediately. He had been asleep! He must not have realized that we needed him to drift to the end of the reef with us and had taken a nap as he waited for us to reappear from the depths. He immediately started the motor and headed toward us. As we were now already a few hundred feet off the island, we started swimming toward the boat. We quickly real-ized that the current seemed a lot stronger when we were trying to swim *against* it than when we were just drifting along with it. Even with scuba fins on, we made absolutely no headway but more or less held our ground.

The boat was within about three-quarters of a mile of us when all of a sudden it swung back toward the island. We could not believe our eyes! He was not going to pick us up! Then, over the water, we heard the outboard sputtering, almost dying, then surging back to life to run steady for a few seconds, only to repeat the sequence. To anyone with much experience with outboard boat motors, this could mean only one thing. The dive boat was running out of gas! We all inwardly groaned. This meant the boat would not get back to us until we were at least a mile offshore. It is not fun drifting out to sea when it is starting to get dark. As we watched the boat sputter back toward the island, we were not frightened though.

Most of us were involved with the sea in one form or another; several of us were budding marine scientists. A group dynamic quickly materialized. We needed to remain calm and stay put so we could be rescued. That was the point at which we decided to drop our tanks and swim against the current to hold our position until the boat got back to us. I thought I was the only one who saw a shadow pass over my tank as it spiraled down. I said nothing so as not to alarm the other members of the group. I found out later that at least one other member saw the same thing but also decided not to tell the group. In retrospect this was probably a good thing. If each of us thought that no one else saw it, then maybe it did not really happen, at least not the way it was perceived. However, if two people saw the same thing that would suggest that something big (hell, something would have to be HUGE to take a scuba tank in its mouth) really was down there, and it was hungry.

As we struggled against the current, we started to spread out and separate from each other. I realized this was a bad thing. We needed to stay together, if for no other reason than to look like one big scary sea monster to whatever was down there munching on scuba tanks. It was now truly starting to get dark. Giving up trying to swim, we formed a floating ring, interlocking our arms. The current slowed as we drifted and bobbed away from the island, but it was still quite strong, two knots at least. We could see the twinkling lights start to go on all over Carriacou. Minutes passed by. Where the hell was the dive boat?! Then, we could see several boats coming toward us. They had lights and were weaving back and forth as they made their way in our direction, searching for us. The problem was that the search boats were only about one mile off the island, and we were at least three miles off shore and still drifting steadily away. We yelled until we were hoarse. A few of the guys had tiny dive lights useful for looking into reef crevices, but they were too weak to be seen from several miles away, even in the late twilight. We watched the boats get smaller and smaller in the fading light, until they were just pinpoints of lights, dancing in the distance.

This is when the reality of our situation hit us. We were truly drifting out to sea. We could not believe our bad luck. We cursed the dive-boat operator over and over. Australians can come up with the most amazing strings of curse words. All of this, of course, did not help our state of affairs. We figured that with a two-knot current we would be about 15 miles from Carriacou by daybreak. We thought the current would take us east of Grenada, but the wind was simultaneously blowing us to the west, so perhaps we would end up on Grenada. We found out later that the tide was already taking us west of Grenada, and the wind was just blowing us even further away from the path to Grenada. We did not realize it, but our next landfall was probably going to be Venezuela, South America, about 150 miles away. If we were lucky, we would hit Trinidad or Tobago, a mere 90 miles from our position.

Although we were all hungry and starting to get a bit thirsty, our real problem was exposure. Most members of the group were wearing some type of wetsuit. I and one other guy were not. It is very hard for me to get chilled, but my teeth were starting to chatter after three hours in the sea. To keep our spirits up and try to help stay warm, we started doing goofy things, like telling bad jokes and teaching each other drinking songs. From my experience as a bartender, I had lots of bad jokes to tell. I did not have much in the way of drinking songs to contribute, but the English and Swedish guys had a about a million, some of which should not be repeated in polite company. Americans just do not tend to sing when they drink.

Finally, though, it was impossible to overcome our depression at being lost at sea. It was now approaching midnight, and we knew it was going to be a long five hours until daybreak. At this realization, the group lapsed into silence, each person seemingly lost in his own thoughts. At this point it is unlikely that anybody truly believed that we were going to die out there in the Caribbean Sea. We all had buoyancy compensators, so staying afloat was not a problem. There were a lot of boats traveling between the islands, weren't there?

I tried to remember how many boats I had seen during my stints at the wheel on the sailboat and motor yacht. Quite a few, but sometimes there were hours between sightings. And more importantly, would I have noticed a group of six people floating in the water? Probably not, unless I was just about ready to run them over. I thought about the difference between riding over the waves in a boat with some type of propulsion and bobbing in the waves, being taken wherever the wind and current sent you. Probably the biggest difference was in the level of noise. Even in a sailboat, the sails snap and sometimes hum in the wind. The boat itself creaks and groans as it slices through the waves. The steady pulse of the engine in a motor yacht is a constant assault on, or comfort to, the ears, depending on whether one has recently had engine problems or not. Bobbing in the ocean, all one hears is the gentle splash of waves as they hit against the buoyancy compensators or when someone shifts an arm position. I found out that it can be very, very quiet at sea.

I again thought about what might be down below. I had seen the movie *Jaws* a few years back. I considered it one of the most suspenseful movies I had ever seen, especially when the dunh-dunh, dunh-dunh music started. That music signaled that the shark was about to attack or at least arrive on the scene. Dunh-dunh, dunh-dunh. I swore that I could hear it again, right there in the water, as I drifted to South America with my legs dangling down like some kind of hairy bait. My imagination was obviously working overtime. No, wait. I *did* hear something! Was Jaws coming?! No, this was more of a thrum, thrum type of sound. Now the other members of our group started to hear it too. The floating ring picked up some life, becoming animated. Something was definitely heading our way, but we could not see it. It was definitely a boat, probably a big boat judging by the deep sound of the engine, but where was it? Why were there no lights? Suddenly, we could see it. The waves being thrown off the bow sparkled with phosphorescence, enabling us to see the boat. It was coming our way; it would pass within about a hundred meters of us! We waved, shouted, screamed, and flashed our small dive lights. The boat did not seem to notice, did not waver in its course. It was going to pass us by! The two people with the dive lights began launching themselves as high as possible out of the water and falling back in, making their own phosphorescent signal. We seemed to be making enough noise and commotion to wake the heavens. I vaguely wondered if this would attract sharks . . .

The boat was now abreast of us, still continuing its steady engine drone with no lights, no signs of life on board. I realized with a sinking feeling that the boat was going to pass us by. No, wait, the engine sound changed. It slowed down, then throttled back completely to an idle. The boat turned upwind and hove-to. A large search beam shot out from the boat, going over our heads. We continued waving and jumping and screaming, and the beam slowly lowered. There! We were in the searchlight's beam! We were saved!

A harsh voice called out from the boat. We all responded at once, screaming and yelling for them to pick us up. The engine noise changed slightly and the bow slowly swung in our direction. They were coming for us! We stopped screaming but kept waving our arms and lights. The boat pulled up next to us, within about fifty feet, and the engine cut back again. We started to swim toward the boat. Again a harsh voice called out. Now we realized that the voice was in some foreign language, we thought probably Spanish. One member of our group who apparently knew Spanish yelled back. The harsh voice called out again. Our newly deputized Spanish interpreter hesitated. We all stopped swimming. Something in the sound of the voice did not sound friendly. "I don't understand him," our interpreter said. "I think he is talking Portuguese or something."

At that point another member of our group, who apparently had not been paying much attention to the exchange (which made him an idiot in my humble opinion) but did have some high school Portuguese (which made him a hero in my humble opinion), started yelling a phrase over and over. The only word I thought I could recognize was "Carriacou." The voice on the boat responded. Our newly deputized Portuguese interpreter idiot-hero said, emotion cracking his voice, "I don't think they want to pick us up. They don't want us on the boat. I think maybe they are drug smugglers or something, coming up from Brazil."

Drug smugglers! That would explain the lack of running lights in the open ocean at midnight! Not pick us up! What could we do to convince them to take us back to Carriacou?! "Tell them we will pay them lots of money if they take us back," someone in the group suggested.

Our interpreter started to yell something to the boat but was quickly cut off. He said, "I think they don't want to wait around for us to go get them money when we get back to the island. I think they are illegal [yeah, duh!] and do not want to be seen near an island during daylight."

At this point we had been slowly moving toward the boat, more or less doggy paddling toward the light, which kept a steady, unblinking eye on us. "Hey, mate, offer them our dive watches! They're worth a lot of money!" one of the Australians called out. Or was it the English guy? Either way, this sounded like a great idea to me, especially since I did not have a watch to lose.

Our interpreter called out something. There was no answer for a few seconds, and then the boat voice said something reluctantly.

"I think he wants to see the watches. Who's got a dive watch? Show it to them." Two of our group started swimming closer to the boat, then reaching toward their wrists as they removed their watches and held them high in the light. Only two watches! Was this enough to pay for the passage of six people?

Apparently, the smugglers really just needed an excuse to pick us up, because the next thing we knew, a kind of rope ladder thing was dropped over the side. We immediately swam toward it. We were being saved! As the first of our group grabbed the ladder, there was a flurry of activity up on deck. The first person reached the top of the ladder and was suddenly yanked up out of sight into the darkness past the deck rail. Something did not seem completely right, but I figured since there was no yelling or signs of violence that being on the boat was immeasurably better then being in the water. When it was my turn to climb the ladder, I deflated my buoyancy compensator, took off my fins and slid them up my arm as the others had done, and started up the ladder. The sea released me reluctantly, the pull of gravity now heavy and seemingly trying to force me back into the water. I struggled upward, and as I reached the top, strong, rough hands shot out and pulled me into the boat, then shoved me down on the deck into some type of cave. I realized I had been shoved under a big sail or more likely a canvas tarpaulin, judging by its roughness. I just lay there, panting and dripping alongside my dive buddies, overcome by gravity and wondering what was going to happen next. The next member of our group was shoved in beside me, and finally the last member was on board and covered by the tarp. The engine noise immediately increased in volume, and we could feel the boat getting underway.

Even though it was stifling lying under the tarp, it was pretty obvious to us that the smugglers were not going to allow us to sit on deck, see their faces, or in any way compromise their clandestine journey. At first the closeness of our bodies and subsequent trapped body heat felt good after shivering in the sea for so long, but we soon became overheated in the warm tropical night. It was damp, hot, and hard to breath, but we did not care. We were heading back toward Carriacou (we hoped), and that was all that mattered.

The boat seemed to drone on for hours, but it was probably more like forty minutes. We could not tell how long because we no longer had any watches. Someone mentioned that they had to go to the bathroom. "You should have pissed in the water when you had the chance," someone else responded. For some reason this seemed hysterical to all of us, and we started laughing. We, of course, had all been peeing in the water over the course of the night. It was the only way to give ourselves a warm feeling out there in the chilly sea . . .

Suddenly the engine cut back. The edge of the blanket was lifted up, and a voice spoke in what we now knew to be Portuguese. Over the shoulder of the smuggler, we could see the twinkling lights of an island. Was that Carriacou?

"I think he says they are not going to stop. We have to jump off the boat and swim in."

Jump and swim? No problem! We had all done dive entries from boats—just not *moving* boats. Hey, if the U.S. Navy SEALs could do it, then we could. At this point nothing seemed to matter except getting back on dry land. I perched on the edge of the deck, putting on my mask and fins. Looking up, I saw a blurry ring of smuggler faces. One seemed to have a smile on his face. Hopefully, it was because he had done a good deed and not because they had tricked us and were dropping us off on some other island. Standing up, I pushed my mask tightly to my face and took a giant step forward. I hit the water harder than expected, and the cold water added to the shock. The boat was apparently still going pretty fast. I cleared the water from my mask and looked around. My dive buddies were already swimming toward the island. It looked to be about a half mile away. I could not tell where we were but it did not matter. Swim toward the lights and figure where we were later. Hopefully there was no coral to scrape on between us and land.

Fueled mostly by adrenalin, we flippered on. We could now see breakers. Was it a reef or a rocky shoreline? We got closer. It was a beach! A beautiful, sandy beach with beach chairs sitting out in the starlight, waiting for us! We recognized the beach as belonging to one of the hotels on the island. We were back on Carriacou! After resting in the chairs in numbed silence for a while, we dragged ourselves back to our respective accommodations. I got the house key out from under the bougainvillea pot on the back porch, let myself into the house, and went to my room. I collapsed on the bed. I had had enough adventure for one night.

The rest of my spring break was not quite as eventful. The dive tender was fired, but I found out later he was rehired as soon as our entire group left Carriacou. Five of the six scuba tanks were eventually recovered by the dive shop. Whether mine was the one missing, I will never know for sure, but I would not have been surprised if it were. After spending so much time in the water, the thrill of diving Carriacou was gone, and I left the island two days after our adventure. Before I left I got the addresses of the two dive-watch owners, so I could mail money to each to help cover their replacement cost. I considered it a small price to pay for getting out of the sea and back on land.

My trip back to the West Indies Lab went a bit less smoothly than my trip down-island. My doctor sponsor connected me with a boat going all the way to Martinique, but there I stalled. No one was heading further north. After hanging around the marinas for two days, I finally ended up having to sell some of my clothes to buy passage on a steamer from Martinique to St. Martin. This was the era of designer jeans, so the fact that Gloria Vanderbilt's name was stitched on the ass of the jeans made them valuable on a Caribbean island with no malls. I sold them on the beach in twenty minutes. My West Indies Lab T-shirts brought good money too because they had cool silkscreen designs and were obviously very unique.

I got to St. Martin the day before classes were starting at WIL. How to get back to school? I finally lucked out again because a water tanker was leaving St. Martin for St. Croix, and they would give me a ride for only twenty dollars! It was not leaving for another day, but I figured better late than never. Anyway, everyone knows that nothing important happens the first day back from spring break.

We docked at the Christiansted dock on St. Croix, and I hitchhiked the nine miles out to the West Indies Lab. I got there just after lunchtime. As I walked into my dorm room, I saw Andy Romano lying on his bed, eyes closed, and wearing a Yankee cap. As I walked up to my bunk, he opened one eye.

"I got to meet Bucky Dent," he said. "It was cool! Da Yankees are gonna take da pennant! Hows was your break?"

"I went down-island. I got as far as Carriacou. I saw a shark eat my scuba tank," I said.

"Cool!" he said, closing his eye.

Additional Readings

Gladfelter, W. B. 1988. *Tropical marine organisms and communities.* St. Croix, V.I.: Argus Publishing.

Gladfelter, E. H. 2002. *Agassiz's legacy: Scientists' reflections on the value of field experience.* Oxford: Oxford University Press.

The Hunt for Public Germs

DAVID GILMORE

◈ ALTHOUGH I AM an environmental microbiologist, I do most of my research at my lab bench rather than out in the field, only occasionally venturing outside to collect environmental samples and culture microorganisms from them. On this occasion, I ventured out on behalf of the local TV station. It seems that one of their reporters is "germophobic." Whenever she picks up silverware in a restaurant, shakes a hand, or, especially, handles money, she can't stop from thinking about what germs she might be handling.

It's true, to some extent, of course: germs are everywhere. Specifically, there are bacteria in water, in soil, on our skin, and in our mouths that are constantly being spread about by wind, touch, coughing, and speaking. Most are harmless under all conditions, and the others cause harm only under certain conditions. Viruses are also found where people have been. They are easily spread about and can "survive," to the extent viruses are alive in the first place, on inanimate objects. When you handle these objects with your fingers, you are likely to inoculate yourself or the food you eat. A virus that you pick up this way is much more likely to cause a minor illness, but is much more difficult to find and identify because of the special conditions needed to grow viruses.

The urge to teach and a respect for the truth are common characteristics of a university professor, so, fearful of a possible tendency toward sensationalism on the part of the news media, I made sure the reporter knew that we just couldn't show the presence of the viruses even though they were more likely to cause disease. We certainly could, however, show that there were bacteria present and even look for some that the average TV viewer would recognize, such as *Escherichia coli* and *Staphylococcus aureus.* It sounded good enough to her. I was interested in my sixty seconds of fame, even if it would only be fame to the viewers of the local TV news, and I agreed to accompany the reporter and her camera person and help them hunt for infamous bacteria among the frequently touched objects found in public places.

The plan was straightforward. After obtaining permission from a business to do sampling and interview people, the reporter asked people if they ever thought about germs while handling money ("No, not really" was a common response) while I sampled money and other objects with swabs which I then dropped into culture media. All was captured by the ever-attentive eye of the TV camera, creating an audiovisual record to be carefully edited into a news story.

We sampled everything from money at a convenience store to a public pay phone and a restroom in the Lab Sciences building on campus. "Germs in our kitchens" was another popular concern, so we paid a quick visit to the camera person's apartment to look for bacteria lurking there. Finally, we descended on headquarters: the TV station's building. Is the rim of that vending-machine soda can that you're about to put your mouth on really clean? We also swabbed a telephone and a computer keyboard to see what the TV staff might have left there.

All the samples were brought back to the lab and incubated. A few simple tests were done to try and differentiate *E. coli* and *S. aureus* from the other bacteria. One result was unsurprising: bacteria were everywhere. Money, the pay phone, a kitchen towel, and even the lip of the soda can had something on it that could be cultured. Scientists tell us that the world is full of unculturable bacteria that our methods would never have found, so bacteria were probably in all those places whether we could grow them or not.

Were there dangerous bacteria lurking out there? *E. coli* didn't turn up. Some of its close relatives were found in the restroom, but not *E. coli* itself. Antibiotic-resistant *Staph aureus* is in the news more and more, and any *Staph aureus* we might find could potentially be among these difficult-to-kill bacteria. Were they on the money? Pay phone? Toilet seat? Soda-can lip? Nah. We found *Staph aureus* in the office of the TV station! Both the telephone and computer keyboard came up positive. It must be tough to be germophobic when the most potentially dangerous bacteria live where you work.

I taped my sixty seconds of fame out in the field. I'll have to pull it out and watch it again sometime.

Additional Readings

Rutala, W. A., E. B. Setzer Katz, R. J. Sherertz, and F. A. Sarubbi Jr. 1983. Environmental study of methicillin-resistant *Staphylococcus aureus* epidemic in a burn unit. *Journal of Clinical Microbiology* 18(3):683–688.

Williams, A. P., L. M. Avery, K. Killham, and D. L. Jones. 2005. Persistence of *Escherichia coli* O157 on farm surfaces under different environmental conditions. *Journal of Applied Microbiology* 98(5):1075–1083.

The Sears Craftsman Wooden-Handled, Four-Pronged Potato Rake

STANLEY TRAUTH

🐉 WHAT'S THE MOST essential tool for any field biologist, especially a herpetologist, to possess? It is a tool for lifting rocks, turning rotting logs, and, as I discovered, digging lizards out of their winter burrows. The four-pronged potato rake is the ideal tool for these uses, but not just any potato rake will do. I have purchased many potato rakes over the course of my thirty-five years of studying amphibians and reptiles, and only one potato rake can withstand the use and abuse inflicted by a field herpetologist. Only one potato rake can flip sixty- and eighty-pound rocks without breaking a tine or its handle. That special, essential potato rake is the Sears Craftsman wooden-handled, four-pronged potato rake.

I always tell my students in herpetology and natural history that this is the tool they need to purchase. Students, however, in an attempt to save money, first buy the cheaper brands; then when those break on the first field trip, they make the trip to Sears to purchase the real thing.

I first discovered the utility of the potato rake just prior to beginning my doctorate at Auburn University. I was planning to study the reproduction and demography of *Aspidoscelis sexlineata,* the six-lined racerunner. As their name implies, these lizards are almost impossible to catch by hand. I had previously used a noose on the end of a fishing pole to catch collared lizards, but because of habitat differences for the two species, that technique didn't work for capturing racerunners. I tried using bird shot and a 22 pistol, but hitting a green target moving through green weeds

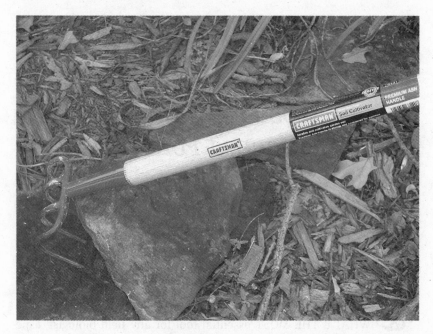

The authentic Sears Craftsman wooden-handled,
four-pronged potato rake.
PHOTOGRAPH BY STANLEY TRAUTH.

and grasses wasn't always possible, and the moving target wasn't the only problem that I encountered. Since roadside clay banks make ideal racerunner habitat, I often walked along the sides of highways with my pistol drawn. Twice in one year, once in Arkansas and once in Missouri, local law enforcement officials asked me to follow them to their offices so they could run the serial number on my pistol.

In the fall of the same year, after the weather had turned cool and the lizards were no longer active, I stopped at a clay bank outside Fayetteville, Arkansas, and for no particular reason, I decided to dig around in the clay. Lizards began to tumble out of their hibernation burrows. I knew I was finished sitting in sheriffs' offices and hunting lizards in the summer when they were active. I could recognize the kind of clay roadside banks that *A. sexlineata* was likely to inhabit, and now I knew that I could dig their cold, lethargic bodies out of their hibernation burrows in the winter even when the ground was covered with snow. My potato rake and I were an immediate success. I became so good at recognizing *A. sexlineata* habitat that at two out of three locations, I would hit a lizard burrow with the first dig of the potato rake. I ultimately dug over two thousand six-lined racerunners out of their burrows in twenty-two states. In south Texas I discovered a previously undescribed subspecies of *A. sexlineata,* now *A. sexlineata stephensae,* which I named after my mother-in-law because she had generously provided funding for me to visit south Texas.

I also discovered that if I picked the correct site, I could dig out *A. sexlineata* eggs during the spring and summer months. Once in Alabama I dug out a clutch of southern fence lizard eggs that were being phagocytized by sarcophagid fly larvae. I later found additional clutches in Arkansas that were being consumed by larvae of the same fly; I found one clutch on Petit Jean Mountain and a clutch at the same site in Randolph County on the same date in two consecutive years.

Since I was now consistently able to dig out clutches of lizard eggs, I decided to investigate whether or not lizard eggs were being phagocytized by the red imported fire ants in Alabama. I dug up thirty-six clutches of

The Sears Craftsman potato rake and a bag of cold, lethargic racerunners just removed from their hibernation burrow. The burrow is visible just to the right of the bag.
PHOTOGRAPH BY STANLEY TRAUTH.

lizard eggs, which I coated with radioactive phosphorus. I selected an abandoned field that had fire ant mounds in it. With my potato rake, I dug out artificial nest chambers and arranged the egg clutches in six groups of six clutches each. I protected the groups of clutches with predator-proof cages, which would still permit fire ants to enter. I waited for two days; then with my long-handled potato rake, I dug up the nearby fire ant mounds. I removed the fire ant larvae and took them back to the lab, where they were tested for radioactivity. They tested positive. This work was published in the *Journal of the Alabama Academy of Science*. I later published other papers on nesting habitat and hibernation in other species of lizards, all made possible by my Sears Craftsman potato rake.

Since those early days of my career in Alabama, I have received numerous grants for herpetological surveys of national parks, wildlife refuges, and military installations. Much of that survey work has been accomplished by groups of students armed with Craftsman potato rakes turning over countless rocks, logs, and pieces of debris. The potato rake can also be used to quickly pen any snake that may be exposed when a

Stanley Trauth today with one of his Craftsman potato rakes
at a typical *A. sexlineata* rocky, clay bank.
PHOTOGRAPH BY JOY TRAUTH.

rock is lifted. Today I always carry in my Suburban three Sears Craftsman wooden-handled, four-pronged potato rakes tucked snugly inside a PVC pipe. I want to be prepared if a snake crosses the road in front of me or a rock needs turning over.

Additional Readings

Mount, R. H., S. E. Trauth, and W. H. Mason. 1981. Predation by the red imported fire ant, *Solenopsis invicta* (Hymenoptera: Formicidae), on the eggs of the lizard *Cnemidophorus sexlineatus* (Squamata: Teiidae). *Journal of the Alabama Academy of Science* 52:66–70.

Trauth, S. E. 1977. Winter collection of *Cnemidophorus sexlineatus* eggs from Arkansas. *Herpetological Review* 8:33.

———. 1983. Nesting habitat and reproductive characteristics of the lizard *Cnemidophorus sexlineatus* (Lacertilia: Teiidae). *American Midland Naturalist* 109:289–299.

———. 1985. Nest, egg, and hatchlings of the Mediterranean gecko, *Hemidactylus turcicus* (Sauria: Gekkonidae), from Texas. *Southwestern Naturalist* 30:309–310.

———. 1987. Natural nests and egg clutches of the Texas spotted whiptail, *Cnemidophorus gularis gularis* (Sauria: Teiidae) from northcentral Texas. *Southwestern Naturalist* 32:279–281.

———. 1988. Egg clutches of the Ouachita dusky salamander, *Desmognathus brimleyorum* (Caudata: Plethodontidae), collected in Arkansas during a summer drought. *Southwestern Naturalist* 33:234–236.

———. 1992. A new subspecies of six-lined racerunner, *Cnemidophorus sexlineatus* (Sauria: Teiidae), from southern Texas. *Texas Journal of Science* 44:437–443.

Trauth, S. E., and G. R. Mullen. 1990. Additional observations on sarcophagid fly infestations of *Sceloporus undulatus* (Sauria: Iguanidae) egg clutches in Arkansas. *Southwestern Naturalist* 35:97–98.

Kind of Blue—It's All about the Name

STARIA VANDERPOOL

"KIND OF BLUE" can be used to describe cross-genre music, moods, or my husband's description of the shirt he's trying to match to a tie, but when I hear the phrase over the phone, I know I'm in for a long, frustrating session with some potential for embarrassment. Someone has called about an unknown plant flowering in their lawn, pasture, ditch, field, or forest, and they want to know what they have. Actually, what they really want me to do is a phone identification of an unknown plant without the fuss and bother of bringing in a specimen to the lab—so they'll call from Jonesboro, Bono, or more distant parts of Arkansas. After all, I teach classes for the Master Gardeners Program; I'm a plant taxonomist, a member of the Arkansas Native Plant Society, and sometimes known as "the gardening lady." I should know all the 2,707 (+) species of vascular plants in the state, plus an additional 200 or 300 species and cultivars of ornamental plants. Right? Wrong! There are several people in the state who can come close, but I can't. However, I'll do my best.

So, . . . the phone rings in my office, I glance up to see that the call is coming from our departmental secretary. I answer it with about half my attention still on the current project. Then I hear some version of the following, "I called the department about this strange plant I found, and they said you could help me." Professional pride, courtesy, and my conviction that I work for the taxpayers who support Arkansas State University demands that I respond. I always ask if they can bring the plant in to the lab for me to identify, but they're convinced that this is such an unusual plant that I can do a phone diagnosis. So, we play "Twenty Questions" as

I desperately try to develop a mental image of their plant (and then a name).

1. What time of the year is it? (Actually, this is a mental question because even I usually know what season it is, but it is important because this narrows down the possibilities.)
2. Where did you find it?
3. What are some of the other plants around it?
4. Is it a tree, shrub, or herbaceous plant?
5. How tall is it?
6. What color is the flower?
7. Are the leaves grasslike or broad leaves?
8. Are the leaves simple or compound?
9. Are the leaves on the stem opposite, alternate, all at the base, or are there leaves present at all?
10. Does it have a distinctive odor? Is it mint-like, pleasant, musty (the technical term is "fetid"), or acrid?
11. Does it look like a pea or bean flower?
12. Does it look like a daisy or sunflower?
13. Does it have a saucer-shaped bloom or is it shaped like a trumpet?

You get the general idea. In the worst-case scenario the answers to these questions stack up like the following: It's mid-spring and this unknown flower popped up along the edge of their lawn, next to the road, or in the woods next to a field. It must be rare; they've never seen it before. It is short and soft-stemmed, the flower color is sort of blue, the leaves are weird looking, the flower smells good, and they think the flower is more like a saucer, but not quite, maybe more like a bowl. But, it's really pretty! What is it? The chances are pretty good that I am not going to successfully answer that question.

One resource I keep in my office that is particularly useful in working with non-taxonomists is *Wildflowers of Arkansas* by Carl Hunter. It is well illustrated and widely used as a convenient reference to showy common wildflowers. Of the 484 species illustrated, approximately 110 are "bluish" (violet through blue and purple). The key phrase above is *illustrated*. In its 2006 guide to vascular plants of Arkansas, the Arkansas Vascular Flora Committee lists 2,896 taxa of plants in the state (191 families, 924 genera, and 2,707 species), and the number grows daily as plant biologists of the state complete comprehensive field and herbarium research as part of the project to produce a comprehensive illustrated manual of the flora of Arkansas.

Based on species numbers alone, there is an 18 percent chance that there is a photograph of the plant in question in *Wildflowers of Arkansas* and an 82 percent chance that there isn't. *Keys to the Flora of Arkansas* by Edwin Smith is the only other guide to statewide flora; it lists 2,518 taxa (distributed among 157 families) for the state. Since Smith's work (1994) and Hunter's work (1995) were published, our research has documented 378 new species in the state that are not represented in *any* of the other readily available resources.

An additional complication arises when the potential pool of possible species is expanded to include cultivated plants. In addition to common "bluish" flowering plants such as hyacinths, bluebells, periwinkle, crocus, and grape hyacinth, there are a tremendous number of uncommon ornamentals such as *Scilla, Ipheion, Broadiaea, Myosotis, Platycodon,* and *Campanula* species and cultivars. I can't venture a guess regarding the number of ornamental taxa potentially hardy in Arkansas, but this unknown number reduces the chance that I, local plant taxonomist extraordinaire, will be able to satisfactorily resolve the caller's question.

Ornamental plants are even more challenging for me when I'm working with the plant enthusiasts, especially gardeners. As a taxonomist, I'm interested in biodiversity, variability among native plants, and characteristics of plant populations. My interest doesn't extend to a concentration on one taxon or the cultivars of a single taxon such as the daylily or bearded iris. When you examine a catalog or visit a nursery, you discover hundreds of cultivars—which the enthusiasts know by name, such as the 1,500 named peony cultivars listed by the Peony Society. While on the garden club circuit as a lecturer when I lived in North Dakota, I encountered this problem.

One of the garden club members had brought a specimen of a *Clematis* (clematis) plant to one meeting and asked me if I could help her identify it. Based on the specimen, I thought this one was easy and promptly answered clematis, which was not the right answer. She then told me that she had over thirty cultivars of clematis in her garden. This was one that had arrived via mail order, and she was convinced that it wasn't the cultivar that she had ordered; she wanted me to tell her what specific cultivar she had, which I was unable to do. I don't think she was impressed by the lecturer's competence that day.

Seriously, gardeners and plant enthusiasts are wonderful people and typically have tremendous knowledge of plants, particularly enthusiasts who concentrate on a specific group, such as iris, peony, rose, or narcissus (also known as daffodil, jonquil, March flowers, and buttercups).

Their understanding of cultivation requirements, soil conditions, exposure, and other ornamental plants is impressive. Even though I garden, I don't have the time or interest to concentrate on a specific group, and my gardening efforts are focused in other areas such as native plants or medicinal plants. I am perfectly happy to have a mixed bed of daffodils and narcissus, and it doesn't bother me that I don't know whether I have a Quail, an Apricot Whirl, a Carlton, a Fortissimo, or a Tropical Sunset cultivar. I think in terms of yellow, white, single or multiple blossoms, and other collective features.

As in so many areas, the problem arises because there are two groups of specialists working with the same biological organisms—flowering plants that have names. Gardeners, native plant enthusiasts, and plant taxonomists speak different languages—literally and figuratively. Throw in someone like me, an absent-minded type who spends a huge amount of time thinking about plants in general, and the potential for miscommunication is tremendous.

When ASU was developing the Hemingway-Pfeiffer Museum and Educational Center in Piggott, Arkansas, I went to the grand opening. While I stood in the audience listening to various state and university visitors speak, the large willow oak outside the front entrance captured my attention. I was reflecting on that tree, the presence of willow oak in the southeast, and other oaks that were symbolic of the south such as the live oak. I had gotten as far as "live oak" in this daydream, when one of my colleagues noticed that I was looking at the tree. He whispered, "What kind of tree is that?" and the first thing that popped out of my mouth was "live oak." He nodded, but looked at me a little oddly, and I went back to thinking deep thoughts about southern history and symbols. Eventually, I woke up, realized that I had thought "willow oak," but said "live oak." I tracked my colleague down and told him that it was willow oak, not live oak. However, I think his faith in my knowledge of trees had definitely been shaken.

Had I been thinking in taxonomic terms rather than literary and symbolic terms, I might not have made that particular error: plant taxonomists tend to think of plants by their scientific name rather than the common name. I would never confuse someone by calling a tree *Quercus phellos* (willow oak) instead of *Quercus virginiana* (southern live oak). I also know the difference between live oaks (as a group of evergreen oak species) and the deciduous oak species. Context and usage determines when one is more appropriate than the other.

The scientific name labels the species with a single name, used universally. When scientific names change, it is because research has shown that the nomenclature has to be adjusted, or it is the result of experimental investigation that splits one large genus into two or more or, more rarely, merges two genera to produce a single genus. For example, the venerable genus *Aster* (common name aster) has recently been separated into four genera: *Symphyotrichum, Erybia, Doellingeria,* and *Ionactis.* The large family of Liliaceae (lily family) has been split into fourteen families, including Agavaceae, Alliaceae, Amaryllidaceae, Hyacinthaceae, and Smilacaceae, among others.

Plant and animal species have scientific names applied following rules originally established by Carolus Linnaeus and subsequently modified by plant taxonomists over the past two hundred years. Although based on the Latin binomial system standardized by Linnaeus, plants, prokaryotes, and animals have different sets of rules for the application of scientific names—codified in the International Code of Botanical Nomenclature (ICBN), International Code of Nomenclature of Bacteria, and the International Code of Zoological Nomenclature. Additionally, a fourth code was established specifically for domesticated plants—the International Code of Nomenclature of Cultivated Plants. In botany the specifics of naming plants were laid down at the 1930 International Botanical Congress (IBC), with emendations at subsequent meetings of the IBC.

Encounters with the general public are most hazardous for plant taxonomists when it comes to names of familiar plants. Many people are familiar with the widely established uniform common names for animals—an eastern bluebird and a mountain bluebird, for example. These are usually based on some easily recognized feature of the animal: gray squirrel and red squirrel or mule deer and white-tailed deer. If you're talking with someone about gray squirrels versus red squirrels, for example, everyone has a good understanding of the two species under discussion. It is a different situation when it comes to plants.

Most plants lack common names, or the common name and the scientific name are not logically linked. One that causes me trouble is yet another oak—*Quercus nigra.* A logical common name would seem to be "black oak," but *Quercus nigra* is commonly known as the water oak. Is there a "black oak"? Yes, but the scientific name is *Quercus velutina.* (Black oaks in Arkansas should not be confused with Black Oak Arkansas—a rock band and the Craighead County hometown of John Grisham.) And, just to confuse the issue, both water oak and black oak are placed in the red oak *group!* Does anyone else have a headache? The recently discovered plant *Sabatia arkansana* bears the common name Pelton's rose-gentian, in honor of the native-plant enthusiast John Pelton, who drew Theo Witsell's attention to a population of rose-gentians that was divergent morphologically from other species of *Sabatia* (six total in Arkansas).

Another factor that complicates the naming of plants is the number of taxa as compared to vertebrate animals in Arkansas. In 1986 Douglas James and Joseph Neal listed 366 bird species for Arkansas, while 137 taxa were cited for the herpetofauna of Arkansas. There are few enough squirrels in Arkansas for each species to have a recognized specific common name. For genera of plants with several very similar species, the common name is usually applied at the generic level. The plant genus *Bidens* (Asteraceae; the composite or sunflower or daisy or aster family) has nine taxa known to occur in Arkansas. Of these, five share the same two common names—beggar ticks and stick tights—based on the awns that arm the fruits and stick to clothing, skin, feathers, and fur. Many of the same group are also known as Spanish needles or tickseed sunflowers.

If we look at another family (the Fabaceae, commonly known as the pea, bean, or legume family), we find the common names beggar's lice, stick tights, and tick-trefoil used for seventeen of the eighteen species of *Desmodium* found in Arkansas. So, one problem with identifying and referring to many plant species is the application of a common name at the genus level. Another problem occurs when the same or a very similar common name is applied to two different groups based on a common feature. In the case of *Bidens* and *Desmodium*, they both share the same seed dispersal mechanism, producing seeds (or fruits) that attach tightly to passing biologists, hunters, and other animals.

Collective names for multiple species are one problem. The flip side of that problem is one species with many common names. These are usually plants that have a long history of use by people as a food plant, an herb, or an ornamental plant. They frequently escape and occur as naturalized plants with large ranges that may include continent-wide native and naturalized regions. Ox-eye daisy (*Leucanthemum vulgare*) is an outstanding illustration of this. It is also called moon daisy, dog daisy, whiteweed, and midsummer daisy. It is easily confused with the cultivated Shasta daisy, also a species of *Leucanthemum*, leading to other problems as *Leucanthemum vulgare* is considered an invasive species and a noxious weed in many states, while Shasta daisy is an ornamental plant. As my plant taxonomy students say, "What!" or sometimes, "Whatever!"

The quagmire of names for plants complicates communication between plant taxonomists, animal taxonomists (who can't understand why every plant can't have a unique common name), and all non-taxonomists. It may distort information. And it may lead to the perception of plant taxonomists as taxonomic purists who insist on only using the scientific name as a form of academic snobbery. I know that it creates difficulties with people who are interested in wildcrafting, collecting plants that are thought to have medicinal properties, plants such as St. John's wort (*Hypericum perforatum*). *Hypericum perforatum* is a European species with a long history of use as a mild antidepressant. It is one of the species that has been investigated as an alternative treatment for depression. It can be found in the Arkansas flora as an introduced species. It is the only species that has been evaluated through clinical trials in Europe. There are fourteen native species of *Hypericum* found in Arkansas. Since some species of *Hypericum* are known to cause photosensitivity in cattle and sheep that consume small quantities in grazing, collection and use of *Hypericum* species is of questionable value. Secondary molecules produced by plants (alkaloids, glycosides, and other bioactive molecules) can have beneficial medicinal properties, but production of these molecules can vary with different populations of a single species. Different species in the same genus can produce different chemical compounds. Precise identification of plants harvested for use as food, herbal preparations for internal or external use, and crafts is crucial for anyone planning to "wildcraft" these plant materials.

In one case of mistaken identity, two plants in the same family (Apiaceae: carrot family) appear rather similar and may be found in similar environments. One is the escaped descendent of our familiar carrot. Queen Anne's lace or wild carrot (*Daucus carota*) can be harvested and the root used as a food source, much like the cultivated carrot. The similar spotted cowbane or water hemlock (*Cicuta maculata*) and poison hemlock (*Conium maculatum*) were responsible for approximately 40 percent of the fatalities linked to plant ingestion from 1985 to 1994 according to *Toxic Plants of North America*, by George Burrows and Ronald Tyrl. The hemlocks can also be confused with the native water parsnip (*Sium suave*), which is edible. Of course, none of these are easily confused with those other hemlocks—the eastern hemlock and the Carolina hemlock (*Tsuga canadensis* and *Tsuga caroliniana*)—two evergreen tree species occurring in the eastern United States and occasionally planted as ornamentals.

The text in this chapter doesn't scroll across my mind when the phone rings and someone asks if I can tell them the name of their mystery plant—based on their description alone—but the ramifications do. I may dispel any illusions about my omniscience or sound pedantic about "the name of that plant," but I'd rather be knowledgeable rather than wing it when questions about identity arise. When talking to others about plants, I try to use the scientific name and the common name together and provide written information to support the identification. But I still answer the phone calls and try to answer the caller's questions. You never know when an observant plant lover will provide information that can lead to an increase in our knowledge of Arkansas flora, as in the very recent case of Pelton's rose-gentian (*Sabatia arkansana*).

Additional Readings

Arkansas Vascular Flora Committee. 2006. *Checklist of the vascular plants of Arkansas.* Fayetteville: University of Arkansas Press.

Burrows, G. E., and R. J. Tyrl. 2001. *Toxic plants of North America.* Ames: Iowa State Press.

Hunter, C. G. 1995. *Wildflowers of Arkansas.* Little Rock, AR: Ozark Society Foundation.

Smith, Edwin B. 1994. *Keys to the flora of Arkansas.* Fayetteville: University of Arkansas Press.

Sumner, J. 2000. *The natural history of medicinal plants.* Portland, OR: Timber Press.

About the Authors

James Bednarz received his undergraduate degree in fisheries and wildlife biology from New Mexico State University. He completed a MS degree in animal ecology at Iowa State University and his PhD degree in biology at the University of New Mexico. He has broad interests in ecology and conservation and began his career working on fish and aquatic systems, but later focused his research on birds, mammals, and conservation issues. Most recently, he has conducted research on six continents, emphasizing avian population ecology and conservation. He has published over 120 scholarly works, including peer-reviewed journal articles, monographs, book reviews, book chapters, conference proceedings, and one technical book, and was the editor of the *Journal of Raptor Research* for five years. He has received over $3 million of research grants and typically advises between six and twelve graduate students as a professor of wildlife ecology at Arkansas State University.

Alan Christian became an assistant professor of biological sciences at Arkansas State University in 2004. He is an aquatic ecologist who has been conducting mussel research since 1992. His master's thesis consisted of surveying and characterizing freshwater mussel communities in the lower White River and the lower Cache River in Arkansas. He earned degrees from the University of Wisconsin–Oshkosh (BS), Arkansas State University (MS), and Miami University (PhD) and worked as a postdoctoral researcher at Arkansas State University in the Environmental Sciences Program. He continues to dive and conduct research on freshwater mussels and other aquatic organisms and aquatic ecosystems. He has been the recipient of over $500,000 in grant money from the Arkansas Game and Fish Commission, the U.S. Fish and Wildlife Service, the Federal Highway Works Administration, and the Arkansas Highway and Transportation Department. Part of this grant money has been used to train and employ six graduate students and over ten undergraduate students at ASU in aquatic ecosystem research.

David Gilmore received his undergraduate degree in biochemistry from the University of Maine and Master's and PhD degrees in microbiology from Indiana University and the University of Connecticut, respectively. He has been teaching microbiology and genetics to students at Arkansas State University since 1992. His research interests relate to the interaction of bacteria with their environment and range from the biochemistry of fish pathogens to biodegradable plastic to the prevalence of *Staphylococcus aureus* on healthy humans.

Richard Grippo earned a BS in tropical marine biology in 1977 and a MS in marine ecology in 1981, both from Fairleigh Dickinson University at Madison. He completed his field work studying nocturnal coral reef fishes at FDU's West Indies Laboratory on St. Croix, U.S. Virgin Islands. He earned a PhD in ecology in 1991 with a minor in statistics from Pennsylvania State University, where he studied the physiological effects of acid mine drainage and acid rain on aquatic organisms. While a graduate student, he supplied scientific support to the class-action litigation associated with the *Exxon Valdez* oil spill in Prince William Sound, Alaska. He was awarded the August and Ruth Homeyer Graduate Fellowship Award for Outstanding Senior Graduate Student at Pennsylvania State University in 1991. He joined the faculty of Arkansas State University in 1995 and chaired the committee that developed the proposal for the first PhD program at ASU, in environmental science. He has received over $1,800,000 in research funding in the areas of biomonitoring, bioassessment, and ecological-risk assessment. In 2006 he was awarded the ASU Environmental Sciences Faculty Research Award. His most challenging achievement is his recent completion of a ten-day, ninety-mile, superstrenuous category, backpacking trip in northern New Mexico's Sangre de Cristo Mountains with the Boy Scouts.

John Harris has been an adjunct professor of biological sciences at Arkansas State University since 1990 and has been a research co-advisor or committee member of over ten graduate students at ASU. At his day job, he has worked for the Arkansas Highway and Transportation Department in the Environmental Division since 1980. He earned his degrees from Southern Arkansas University (BS), the University of Louisiana–Monroe (formerly Northeast Louisiana State University) (MS), and the University of Tennessee (PhD). He is the author of numerous articles and reference materials on freshwater mussels in Arkansas.

Tanja McKay became an assistant professor of entomology at Arkansas State University in 2004. She is a veterinary entomologist who has been conducting research since 1994. Her master's thesis consisted of surveying and releasing parasitic wasps that attack houseflies and stable flies in dairy operations in Manitoba, Canada. Her PhD dissertation examined the fascinating oviposition behaviors of *Muscidifurax zaraptor,* a common parasitic wasp of houseflies found in North America. She earned degrees from Acadia University, Wolfville, Nova Scotia (BS), University of Manitoba, Winnipeg, Manitoba (MS), and Kansas State University (PhD). She worked as a post-doctoral researcher at the University of Arkansas, where she surveyed and released parasitic wasps in broiler-breeder and turkey finishing houses in Northwest Arkansas. She also identified pathogens of food-quality importance such as *Campylobacter, Salmonella,* and *Escherichia coli* that are commonly harbored by flies. She has been the recipient of grant money from the U.S. Department of Agriculture, Arkansas Department of Higher Education, and the National Science Foundation.

Fabricio Medina-Bolívar has held a joint appointment as an assistant professor of metabolic engineering in the Department of Biological Sciences and the Arkansas Biosciences Institute at Arkansas State University since 2005. He is a world-recognized expert in the area of plant biotechnology and natural products. He has over fifteen years of experience in the area of plant tissue culture and transgenics with emphasis on the application of hairy roots for the production of natural products and recombinant proteins. He received the 2006 Arthur Neish Award from the Phytochemical Society of North America based on his research contributions to the field of phytochemistry. He has published several peer-reviewed papers and review chapters and has given more than one hundred national and international lectures and presentations in areas of plant biotechnology and natural products. He has been the primary coordinator of two international agreements signed between ASU and CONICET and ASU and Universidad Nacional Agraria in Lima, Peru. He is also co-founder of two biotechnology companies, Nature Diagnostics, Inc. (Blacksburg, Virginia), and Nature West, Inc. (Jonesboro, Arkansas), which focus on molecular/chemical-based diagnostics and production of natural products for the food and pharmaceutical industries, respectively. He received his BS in biology from Cayetano Heredia University (Lima, Peru) in 1992 and PhD in plant physiology from Pennsylvania State University in 1997.

Thomas Risch is an associate professor of wildlife ecology at Arkansas State University. He received a BS in environmental studies from the Richard Stockton College of New Jersey, a MS in wildlife management from Frostburg State University, and a PhD in zoology from Auburn University. His research interests include the evolution of life-history traits and secondary sexual characteristics in birds and mammals and the conservation of threatened and endangered mammals.

Aldemaro Romero obtained his undergraduate degree in biology from the University of Barcelona, Spain, and his PhD in biology from the University of Miami (1984). He is currently chair and professor at the Department of Biological Sciences at Arkansas State University. He has published more than 490 scholarly works, including peer-reviewed manuscripts, articles in non-peer-reviewed publications, books, book reviews, and abstracts. He has obtained numerous research grants as well as teaching, research, and service awards from a variety of public and private agencies in the United States and abroad. He has a broad range of interests that include, but are not limited to, biology of cave organisms (particularly fish), environmental history of marine mammals in the Caribbean, and general scientific issues. His work has included field, laboratory, and theoretical methodologies. Of particular interest to him are intriguing questions in science that require an interdisciplinary approach.

Stanley Trauth has been associated with the Department of Biological Sciences at Arkansas State University since 1984. He is a professor of zoology and currently the director of the ASU Electron Microscope Facility. He received his BS and MS degrees from the University of Arkansas, Fayetteville, and a PhD from Auburn University in Alabama. He has been investigating Arkansas's amphibians and reptiles for nearly thirty-five years and is the senior author of a recent book entitled *The Amphibians and Reptiles of Arkansas.* He is also senior curator of a herpetological collection of over thirty thousand catalogued specimens; he mentors ten graduate students and has received over $550,000 in grants dedicated to herpetology-related projects during the past five years. He has been managing editor or editor-in-chief of the *Journal of the Arkansas Academy of Science* since 1992, and he along with two colleagues recently launched a new electronic journal, *Herpetological Conservation and Biology.* In 2005 he was awarded the ASU Board of Trustees Faculty Award for Scholarship and Research.

Staria Vanderpool received her undergraduate degree in biology from the College of the Ozarks in Missouri, an MS in biology from Arkansas State University, and her PhD in plant taxonomy from the University of Oklahoma in Norman (1989). She is currently assistant professor of botany and curator of the E. L. Richards Herbarium at Arkansas State University, where she continues to work in plant conservation biology and experimental, investigative plant evolutionary biology. In addition to her work in botany, she is active in both formal and informal science education. She and a colleague received National Science Foundation (NSF) funding to develop problem-based learning labs for non-major biology students at ASU, resulting in a new lab text and complete restructuring of the lab infrastructure. Recently, she and other colleagues received NSF funding for a teacher-training program using forensics as an integrating strategy for grades four through twelve. She is faculty sponsor for the National Education Association chapter of Women in Science. With this group she has been involved with informal science education programs targeting fifth-, sixth-, and eighth-grade girls. She continues her public service program with a nine-year term as a commissioner for the Arkansas Natural Heritage Program, instructor for University of Arkansas Extension Coop Master Gardener's Program, and treasurer of the Arkansas Native Plant Society. Recent publications include release of the *Checklist of the Vascular Plants of Arkansas,* the first of a series of works that will result in a manual of the flora of Arkansas produced by the Arkansas Vascular Plant Committee. Her *Investigating Biological Sciences,* 3rd edition, was published in 2005.

Index